THE ASHRAM

A True Story of Enlightenment

and the Dark Night of

the Soul

SOPHIE > MAY THE FORCE
BE WITH YOU!

EB

1·26·2015

ERIC L. BULLARD

The following is a true story of the events that transpired in my life from 1989 to 1999. I have done my best in this account to describe certain events and circumstances that lie beyond the range of normal human, mental, and spiritual experience. To those interested in the subjects of deep meditation, the ancient traditions of India, and the phenomenon of Kundalini, I recommend the reading list at the back of the book. Of particular interest are Gopi Krishna's treatises on the Kundalini force.

The great way is profound, wondrous, and inconceivable, how could its practice be easy? Have you not seen how the ancients gave up their bodies and lives, abandoned their countries, cities and families, looking upon them as shards of tile? After that they passed eons living in the mountains and forests, bodies and minds like dead trees, only then did they unite with the way. Then they could use mountains and rivers for words, raise the wind and rain for a tongue, and explain the great void.

Eihei Dogen

Prologue

*The real voyage of discovery consists not in
seeking new landscapes, but in having new eyes.*
MARCEL PROUST

IN JUNE OF 1983 I was completing a five-month tour
of the South Pacific. One in which I visited several
small island groups and the countries of New Zealand
and Australia. I had worked hard for almost two years
as a cook and a bartender back in the States, sometimes working sixteen hours a day in order to save
money for the trip. And so by the time of departure,
January 1983, I was really looking forward to taking
off, traveling for a bit, relaxing for a while, and seeing some new places and cultures. But throughout my
travels there was something else that I was thinking
about and searching for. At the time I didn't know exactly what it was. All I knew was that there had been
a feeling of disillusionment, tension and dissatisfaction growing within me for the past couple of years,
something I couldn't escape from. It was a feeling, or
rather a sneaking suspicion, that told me there was

something else far more important in life than what I had found so far.

My travels took me first to Hawaii and then to the beaches and highlands of the Fijian Island chain where I lived with the Indigenous natives up in the mountains studying their prehistoric culture that had somehow miraculously survived into the twentieth century. Next I traveled the length and breadth of New Zealand; it's beaches, it's cities, and it's mountains, finally ending up on remote Stewart Island in the Southern Pacific; New Zealand's South Island barely visible almost twenty miles away to the north. In Australia I followed the east coast up to the Great Barrier Reef where I explored various islands, snorkeled the underwater forests of coral reef and relaxed in the ample sunshine. And finally, with time and money running out, I journeyed up to the Blue Mountains just west of Sydney for a final two weeks of hiking and climbing.

Arriving in the Blue Mountains in June of 1983 I almost felt a sense of desperation. Although I'd had a great time those last five months I still felt that same empty, gnawing sensation in the pit of my stomach, now heightened by the knowledge that my vacation was almost over. In a few short weeks I would be going back to the same world I had left behind five months earlier. And so now desperate to find something new, concerned about time and definitely not looking forward to going back to the States without finding that which I had set off in search of, I decided to make those last two weeks in the Blue Mountains of Australia a spiritual retreat. I would climb Mount

Solitaire in the heart of the Blue Mountain Range, sequester myself in a comfortable spot near the summit, fast, pray and wait for guidance or a sign as to what I should do with my life in the years to come.

Deciding all of that, I went into a town on the edge of the park, bought some supplies and then, almost as a second thought, bought two books at a used bookstore for entertainment up on the mountain. The climb up Mount Solitaire was pretty simple, the weather was great and after a short search I found a comfortable camp spot on the broad summit amongst a grove of eucalyptus trees with an excellent view out over the valley and forest below. I spent my days fasting, searching for water, gazing out over the valley below, drinking orange spice tea and reading the two books that I had brought along.

The first book that I read was entertaining enough but it was the second book that really caught my interest. It was about stress and the possibility of living a happier, healthier, more satisfying life through the practice of meditation. I was intrigued and fascinated by the information, theories and case studies in the book. Here at last, I thought, was the thing that I had been searching for: a documented, scientifically proven method that I could practice twice a day on my own time to alleviate stress and bring about a deeper, broader sense of purpose and satisfaction in my life.

Incredible, I remember thinking. So easy, so simple; I had been searching for so long and then there it was all spread out in front of me in black and white. At last, the answer to my dissatisfaction, my doubts, and my growing tension. Now I could go home, learn to meditate and go back to living a real, and hopefully more satisfying life. I finally felt excited for the first time in years and at last ready to end my wandering and searching and head back home to the States. I completed my fast, ate for a few days to regain my strength, hiked out in a pouring rain and then caught the train back to Sydney and a few days later my plane back to America. Back home in Portland, Oregon, I paid two hundred dollars and took a five-day course during which I was initiated into the practice of one of the various forms of meditation that was available in Portland at that time.

The results were unbelievable, far beyond all that I had read about in that book atop Mount Solitaire in Australia. For the first time in years I felt really, truly happy and fulfilled. And more than that, I felt a deep sense of satisfaction and contentment. All of a sudden I was happier and more able than I had ever been in my life. Problems and situations that would have confounded me for days or even weeks previously were now handled in minutes. Work was a breeze, decisions easy, and my relationships with others finally made sense. I was relaxed, centered, charged with calm energy, and nothing could affect me in a negative way. I felt connected to the source.

This state of relaxation, this new state of deep contentment, lasted for about two months and then faded a bit but stayed strong enough over the next year to keep me interested in and focused on my meditation program and the steps that followed: I went to group lectures and group meditations, I got advanced techniques, and I went on meditation courses where we practiced extended hours of yoga asanas and meditation. Learning to meditate was one of the greatest, if not the greatest thing that I had ever done in my life, and the day-to-day results were proving it's worth.

After about a year of immersing myself in this new culture, this new lifestyle, I began hearing about an advanced meditation technique called the Yoga Sutras of Patanjali which was supposed to be one of the most powerful meditation techniques, if not the most powerful, known to exist. I was fascinated reading about it and talking to people who had learned the technique. I then found out that it was possible to learn the technique. It wasn't easy, there was an exhaustive application and screening process, and it was only taught at certain times of the year in distant lands, but it was possible.

There were basically two ways to learn the Yoga Sutras of Patanjali meditation technique. One was to pay an incredible amount of money, go through the application process and fly to one of the specially selected ashrams that the meditation group I was following had spread throughout the world. The second method was to travel directly to one of the ashrams, commit to work there for a year, and then, after six months, apply for and hopefully receive the technique at no cost. Thinking about it all intrigued me. I had been meditating now for over a year and a half, the benefits were substantial and I was curious to see what was next. Why not let it all go, live in a Hindu ashram for a year and take a big look at the other side? I mean, I knew that there was still a lot more to life than living in the United States, working forty hours a week and hoping to get married someday and have kids. I was reading about enlightenment, states of consciousness that transcended pain, death and suffering, people who lived in the Himalayas and knew how to levitate! I wanted to see if it were all really true. I wanted to turn life inside out and see what was really at the center. And more than anything else, I wanted to break out of the Westernized lifestyle and belief system that I felt was still holding me back spiritually.

So it was rather an easy decision for me in 1985 to put all of my possessions into storage at my parent's house, quit my job, and travel far away to a distant mountain top where I committed myself to work for a year completely away from almost everything I had known in life up to that point. I stayed on that mountaintop with seven other people sequestered away from civilization and worked like a dog for six months. I cooked, worked in the fields, cleaned, did my daily meditations and attended knowledge classes in the evening. Slowly but surely, due to the isolation, strength, and focus of the program, I was able to begin to let go of the lifestyle and mental framework that I had known before and start to adopt a new, broader, deeper, perspective and understanding of life.

After six months in the ashram I was granted permission to begin the two-month course in which I would be taught the Yoga Sutras of Patanjali meditation technique. To learn the sutras it was necessary for me to travel four hours away to the city where I would be in direct contact with one of the advanced teachers of the movement. He was the one that was going to teach me, or rather us (we were nine students in all) the technique. And so for the next two months, every weekend, I left the familiar routine of the ashram and journeyed down the mountain to study with this master.

The results of learning the new technique were once again incredible and even more profound than that which I had felt two and a half years earlier when I had been initiated into the basic meditation technique. For in learning this new, profound deep meditation technique totally new realms of happiness, fulfillment, inner vision, and personal satisfaction were immediately made available to me. And it was not because something was happening outside in my life (fame, fortune, etc.) but rather because I was simply closing my eyes twice a day and journeying deep within myself to the source of all creation. At the end of the two-month course, the final two weeks which were in residence at an affiliated ashram, I returned to the mountaintop ashram and basked in the glory of my new meditation-yoga sutra program (which now had been extended in time from twenty minutes to over an hour twice daily) and the beauty of nature that surrounded me.

Four months later I completed my one-year work commitment for the ashram and asked myself, what now, what next? I was really enjoying the ashram lifestyle and felt happier than I had felt in a long time but didn't really want to stay at the mountaintop ashram anymore due to its extreme isolation and limited possibilities. No I needed something new, something beyond all that I had seen and learned so far. I needed something that would be both a continuation and advancement of what had been started three years earlier with the reading of that simple book atop Mount Solitaire in the Blue Mountains of Australia.

It was then that someone told me about another ashram on the other side of the country where there were thousands of people meditating and practicing the Yoga Sutras of Patanjali together in large groups and creating a wonderful wave of peace, harmony and coherence. I was intrigued and asked to learn more. Yes, it was explained to me, there was a big ashram, one of the biggest in the world, out on the plains where large groups of monks, nuns, students and laymen lived, studied, worked, meditated, and practiced the sutras together. There was also a nearby town of like-minded people and an accredited university where I could study the knowledge full-time. There was everything that I could want or need. I could go, live, work, study, practice my new meditation-sutra program in a large group and learn more about meditation and the possibilities for further spiritual growth. The sky was the limit, the possibilities were endless, and heaven itself seemed at my fingertips.

I packed my bags, told my parents to mail some of my things from Portland and took the week-long trip out of the mountains and across the plains to one of the biggest ashrams in the world. Seeing the campus for the first time was quite a shock after all of the isolation and simplicity of the mountain top ashram. But it was true, there were thousands of like-minded people there from all over the world, a college, and a small town nearby full of meditators who knew how to meditate with the yoga sutras. For me it was like arriving in paradise, everything and everyone so calm and serene. And being in the ashram, which was located on the college campus grounds, was like entering heaven itself. There was an air, an ambience, so smooth, so refined, so serene and yet charged with energy that one felt enlightened just being there.

That first day I enrolled in the ashram on campus and joined the work-study program. I would be working in the campus kitchen during the day and studying the knowledge at night. But it was the meditation and practice of the yoga sutras in the large group that was the real payoff. I had heard that practicing your meditation-sutra program in large groups enhanced the effects but I did not expect such deep and profound experiences so fast. Twice daily I entered into one of the group meditation halls on campus where I participated in a meditation and yoga sutra program of one and a half hours with approximately two thousand other people. The results were as predicted and I felt thrilled as I experienced still further, dramatic refinements of perception, inner peace and coherence.

As the years progressed I took courses which consisted of extended hours of meditation and practice of the yoga sutras. I studied the Hindu texts; The Upanishads, The Bhagavad-Gita, The Mahabarata, and the ancient theories of Ghandarva Veda, Stapatya Veda and, of course, the Rig Veda and how they all related to human consciousness. But it was the study of Ayurveda, the science of health, or in layman's terms India's five thousand year old traditional, holistic system of perfect health, that really captured my attention.

The theories and various therapies of Ayurveda fascinated me. It was a natural health system that was based on simple procedures and everyday knowledge that naturally aligned the individual with a state of perfect health; a state of health far beyond that which was usually referred to as "normal" or "well". I went to lectures and read everything I could on the various aspects of Ayurveda. I followed the dietary and lifestyle guidelines and regimens. Over the next two years I did everything I could to soak up as much information on meditation and Ayurveda that I could to advance my spiritual program.

In 1988 my father found out that he was ill with colon cancer. There was no immediate danger of death, and at that point we didn't even know if it was life threatening, but he would have to cut back on his workload and travel for the family publishing business that he had started twenty years earlier. He wanted to know if I would be interested in coming back to Portland and taking over the marketing and sales division of the business until either he got better or I decided that I liked it enough to stay around. I thought about it for a while and decided to accept. First of all because of my concern for my father and the desire to help him and second of all because I was ready for a change. I had been so deeply immersed in living the ashram lifestyle for over three years by then that I was ready to get out for a while, have a look around and see what was going on in the world. And so in the spring of 1988 I left the ashram and returned to Portland, Oregon and the work-a-day world.

Back in Portland I leaped into my new position as Vice-President in charge of Sales and Marketing. I bought a new car, moved into an office and acquired an expense account. I spent the majority of my time either on the phone or traveling a six-state territory selling and promoting our line of camping, climbing, fishing and outdoor guide books. It was a hectic pace, a heavy workload, and quite different from the lifestyle that I had been living the last three years but I was ready for it after so much rest, relaxation and refinement in the ashram. I continued with my practice of the meditation-sutra program and the dietary and lifestyle regimens of the Ayurvedic health-care system that I had learned in the ashram. I even attended lectures and meditation courses in Portland or in California when I was there on one of my many business trips. I truly thought that I was living the best of both worlds; maintaining the standards of health and spiritual integrity that I had learned through my years in the ashram and at the same time living in and working in the material world.

1

THE ASHRAM, 1989

Our normal waking consciousness, rational consciousness as we call it, is but one special type of consciousness, whilst all about it, parted from it by the filmiest of screens, there lie potential forms of consciousness entirely different. We may go through life without suspecting their existence, but apply the requisite stimulus, and at a touch they are there in their completeness. No account of the universe in its totality can be final which leaves these other forms of consciousness quite disregarded.
WILLIAM JAMES

LOOKING BACK ON it now it seems a little strange, but at the time it all made perfect sense. In fact, it made more sense than anything I had ever experienced in life before. It was the summer of 1989 and I had traveled back to the Hindu ashram where I had previously spent three years studying Ayurveda, meditation and an advanced meditation technique known as the Yoga Sutras of Patanjali. I had left the ashram one and a half years earlier to return to my hometown of Portland, Oregon where I had become Vice-President in charge of Sales and Marketing for the family publishing business. But now after a year and a half of constant travel and a heavy workload I was returning to the ashram for month-long intensive meditation course. It was going to be a vacation for me, a retreat of sorts, and a chance to rest up and regroup before taking on the coming heavy Christmas season work load.

My first days back in the ashram were a pleasant relief from my job as a sales executive and I found myself relaxing easily and enjoying the peace and quiet of being on campus again. The course consisted of extended hours of meditation and advanced meditation techniques (the Yoga Sutras of Patanjali) followed by knowledge classes in the evening. I had at that point been meditating for six years and practicing the Yoga Sutras for more than three. And I had been on similar courses before, but never for more than three or four days at a time. But now back at the ashram I was going to be meditating and practicing the Yoga Sutras for up to six hours a day for an entire month! And besides the extended meditation sessions, I was also going to participate in a six month Ayurvedic marma-aroma therapy program, and be taking a new Ayurvedic product called Amrit Prash (a collection of herbs from India), both of which were intended to enhance and deepen the meditation experience. All in all it was looking to be a good, solid month of deep rest and rejuvenation, just what I needed after all of the hard work and travel of the last year and a half.

The first few days of the course were incredible. Each morning I awoke early, bathed, did ten minutes of yoga asanas, and from 7:00 AM until almost noon, went into one of the group meditation halls on campus where I totally immersed myself in my program of meditation and yoga sutras; four hours in total every morning and another two hours in the afternoon. The extended hours of the meditation course were, as always, amazing; so deep, so profound, so clear, and at the same time so peaceful and gentle. It was like one long Sunday morning in bed, resting and relaxing as much as you wanted to without a care in the world. Due to my previous three years of experience at the ashram and my status as a long term practitioner I was totally unsupervised the rest of the day so could roam the campus grounds, go in to town, or just sit in the sun and relax.

Things continued to go along that way for about four days or so but then very suddenly everything began to change and it was kind of strange because, as I said, I had been on courses like this before and knew more or less what to expect. But with the passing of the fourth day of the course the whole experience of the meditation program began to change. Instead of leveling out as I had on other meditation courses, I began to go deeper and deeper into a vast, expanding ocean of profound peace and broadening perception.

Maybe it was the addition of the marma-aroma therapy, or maybe it was the combination of herbs that I was taking, maybe it was just the fact that with the passing of the fourth day of the course I was now beyond all previous experience and entering into totally new territory. I wasn't sure what was going on but it all felt so good, so clear, and so honest that I didn't want to think about it too much. I just wanted to soak up as much of the new energy as I could, as fast as I could, and so continued meditating and basking in the glory of this new level of profound peace and relaxation that I was discovering. Twice daily, I was diving deep into an entirely new subconscious field of possibilities, discovering fresh, new worlds of peace, joy, and intuitive understanding. Emerging hours later I was a changed man.

This new pace of expansion and comprehension was almost unbelievable and I was terribly excited by the fact. After so many years of study, experience, short tastes, false leads, and hopes for a permanent-concrete experience of the Divine I began to realize that if things kept going the way they were going I was going to arrive at something very big before the month was over. I still wasn't sure what that might be, but referring back to my previous experiences, readings, and studies and cross-referencing all of that information with these experiences it was impossible not to realize that something unique was starting to unfold in my practice.

It was beginning to feel as if I were in the daily process of compressing a year's worth of experience, learning and psychological growth into one day. Imagine, learning everything you learned in your tenth, twentieth or fortieth year of existence in a single day! Then imagine that entire process of perception and learning expanding and speeding up at a breathtaking pace into previously unimagined levels of intelligence and wisdom. I was amazed not only by what I was experiencing, but by the speed it was unfolding. I had planned this merely as a time of rest and rejuvenation; but now, due to all that I was doing, I was finding myself in a world that was expanding, accelerating, and changing at a maddening pace. It excited me, it soothed me, it charmed me, and day-by-day it lured me further into a completely new world of exciting possibilities.

With every meditation now I left this relative world behind, diving deep down into previously unexplored states of consciousness entering a whole new world of information and experience. It felt as if I were some sort of "spiritual miner" going down a long, dark mine shaft, past normal thought and awareness into the unexplored bowels of the earth (my unexplored soul, unconscious mind and beyond). Once there I discovered incredible hidden kingdoms, not rooms or shafts mind you, but broad, vast, brilliant kingdoms of unexpected great light, peace, soul expansion and intuitive sacred knowledge. And it all lay within me! In fact, it had always been there silently waiting but unexplored due to my own ignorance and lack of a proper method of exploration. But now that I had the knowledge of its existence and a way to explore it I was not going to miss the precious opportunity that was being presented to me.

Another good analogy would be that of living in a seemingly flat city your entire life and one day coming upon a gigantic skyscraper. Getting into the elevator and going up to the second or third floor, one would get a completely new perspective of the city in which they lived. If one went up to the sixth floor the next day and the twentieth floor the day after that, one's perspective would become much broader, much fuller, not only in regards to one's own city but also in regards to everything that was beyond that city and had never been known to exist! It was the very concrete experience of moving beyond mere horizontal information, knowledge, and its structure, as we know it, into a new vertical source of direct realization and intuitive knowledge, merging with it and returning to a brand new world!

2

CHIAPAS, MEXICO, 1998

*As the hand held before the eye conceals
the greatest mountain, so the little earthly
life hides from the glance the enormous
lights and mysteries of which the world is
full. And he, who can draw it away from
before his eyes, as one draws a hand,
beholds the great shining of inner worlds.*
RABBI NACHMAN OF BRATZLAV

I AM IN a small *colectivo* (vintage Volkswagen bus) surrounded by diminutive, quiet, dark skinned, Spanish-
speaking Mayan Indians. There are about twelve of
us crammed into the *colectivo* and we are slowly
climbing up a pine covered mountain. We weave
back and forth, in and out of a cool, thick fog. Every

fifteen minutes or so we pass a group of twenty or so Indigenous pilgrims in traditional dress carrying lit torches, carrying banners, carrying portraits of the Holy Virgin. They are running up the mountain barefoot, confident in their faith. A light breeze sneaks in through the partially opened window. I close my eyes, I try to sleep, I try to forget.

One hour later we arrive in the town of San Cristobal de Las Casas, colonial gem of Mexico's most southern state of Chiapas. Founded almost 500 years ago, it is now home to 90,000 Mayan, *Mestizo* (people of combined European and Native American descent), and various wandering souls. Two hours north of the Guatemalan border it sits elegantly perched 6,000 feet high in a deep, green bowl surrounded by the steep, pine clad Southern Sierra Mountains. It is mid-morning, the fog has lifted, the sun is shining, and all is infused with a high mountain vitality, freshness and purity. At the bus station on the outskirts of town I flag down one of the numerous darting taxis and ease into the front seat as we weave through the tight corridors and colonial architecture of San Cristobal. We travel twelve blocks or so towards the center of town and then arrive at number fifty-two, Calle Real de Guadalupe.

Exiting the taxi with my bag, I step into a kaleidoscope of swirling color, noise and activity. Without knowing it, I have landed in the middle of the once-a-year Virgin de Guadalupe *fiesta*. Streamers, banners and flags flutter and fly overhead leading the six blocks eastward to the church of the Virgin of Guadalupe while the street itself is jammed with

Mayan Indians, Mexicans and international tourists. Sky rockets explode above, firecrackers sizzle and crackle at every turn and the music from more than half a dozen nearby super-sound systems combine to create a never ending, ever-increasing wall of noise. All around confetti is falling down like rain while down below dogs are barking and *mariachi* bands are parading up and down the street blasting out traditional songs and anthems as the bells of half a dozen nearby churches ring without end. Mexicans, Europeans, Americans, and Mayan Indians from the villages surrounding San Cristobal all mix and mingle together amidst the music, drinking and dancing to create a lively, bubbling, pulsating scene of color, laughter and excitement. To me it all seems like a homecoming, a grand *fiesta* to celebrate my humble arrival in this ancient city of conquistadors.

Crossing the street, I weave my way through the crowd and enter La Posada Casa Real where I rent a modest room for thirty *pesos*. This *posada* (guest house), constructed more than 200 years ago, used to be an elegant colonial home. But time, business and economy have forced it to its knees and transformed it into a mere tourist hotel. Four rooms on the first floor, five more upstairs, each level supporting its own plant covered, sun drenched terrace with a view of the surrounding mountains, it still holds its head up high. I find my room, stow my gear, and go down the stairs, out into the wild street scene once again.

The street is now even more packed than it was when I first arrived. The combined volume of music, rockets and bells ringing has increased as well. It is almost impossible to pass but somehow I manage to squeeze, dart and duck my way westward through the crowd and away from the *fiesta*. Four blocks later, the crowd greatly thinned, I arrive at the *zocalo* (town square) and a diminished level of hoopla. Turning right at the *zocalo* I find and follow Avenue General Urtrilla northward to another church, the *fiesta* now but a faint rumble in the distance. Four blocks later I arrive at the Santa Domingo church and convent complex.

The church and convent grounds of Santo Domingo cover a full four square city blocks. Founded in 1547 by the Obispo Marroquin of the Dominican order of the Spanish Catholic Church, she has seen the tears and prayers of countless pilgrims for almost half a millennium. The main cathedral resembles a small mountain in size, dwarfing the convent, various out buildings, and a scattering of oaks and pines that cover the grounds. Amongst the pines, in the main courtyard, there is a bustling Indigenous market where hundreds of Tzotzil, Tzeltal, Zoque and Chol Indians sell their homemade goods to a never ending parade of international and national tourists. I skirt along the edge of the market, climb a set of stairs, enter into a second courtyard, and find myself staring up at an enormous baroque styled cathedral face, one of the largest, oldest, and most elaborately decorated in the Americas. Seeing the massive wooden doors to the cathedral hanging leisurely half open, I pass through the twenty-foot portals and enter a deep darkness and reverent silence.

Inside the near empty cathedral I need a moment to adjust my eyes to the darkness, but slowly I am able to see objects, pick out saints and angels, as statues and portraits, flying all about me; Jacinto de Polonia, Domingo de Guzman, la Virgin de Rosario and hundreds more fill the cavernous interior and sing silent praise to the Lord. I feel as if I have entered a mountain and am now walking through a gigantic, never ending, dimly lit cave.

As my eyes become fully adjusted to the darkness I can see that everything is gilded in gold. The statues, picture frames, murals and very walls themselves are all covered with a thick, dim, golden glow. Taking a right-hand turn I slowly walk down the rustic wooden planked floor of the main corridor towards the central altar and in doing so pass row after row of ancient wooden pews and a giant golden pulpit hanging ominously from the left-hand wall. Advancing still further, I come to an intersection and see murky passageways branching off to the left and right where huddled groups of Indians gather in the gloom, light candles and pray to the Lord in their native tongue. With each step I feel as if I am travelling back further and further in time to a place when the whole world was sacred, holy and new. The entire scene reeks of sanctity.

Suddenly and without warning the seemingly endless rows of wooden pews come to an abrupt end and I find myself standing in front of a sixty-foot tall altar which in turn sits directly below a 100-foot domed ceiling reminiscent of the Sistine Chapel. Directly ahead of me, twenty feet off the ground, half way up the altar face, sits, or rather stands an antique silver starburst Spanish cross over six feet tall and three feet wide shining like the northern star in the blackness of night. Another twenty feet higher stands a jewel encrusted Jesus Christ praying to the masses below. And topping it all stands yet another angel, sword in hand, the wrath of God painted on his furrowed brow.

Off to the left, down a short corridor, three holy Marys pray for a woeful Jesus Christ tacked and dying on a wooden cross. Off to my right another grand hall, almost as large as the main hall, also topped with a heavenly dome, opens up and stretches out into the gloom. It too is jammed full of saints, angels, statues, murals, virgins, Jesus Christs and more gold than I have ever seen. I stand in the middle of it all feeling dwarfed and insignificant. It is all so big, so grand, so illustrious, and so silent. I slowly cross myself in Catholic fashion, take a seat in one of the pews and begin to pray. I pray for forgiveness for all the sins that I cannot understand. I pray for guidance. I pray for my lost soul. Prayers turn to tears and I begin to weep away in the near empty church. I weep until I can weep no more then fall gratefully asleep on the hard wooden pew surrounded by saints, angels, gold, and God.

3

THE ASHRAM, 1989

There are no unnatural or supernatu-
ral phenomena, only very large gaps in
our knowledge of what is natural......
we should strive to fill those gaps.
EDGAR MITCHELL, APOLLO ASTRONAUT

ACCOMPANYING THE ENTIRE experience was a feeling of deep, reverent humility and a sense of gratitude for all that I was seeing and experiencing. I was pulling back the curtains of the everyday world and peeking into the Sacred, the Divine Kingdom of Heaven, and it was far greater than I could have ever imagined! Suddenly all of my dreams, desires, expectations, and yearnings since childhood were being answered and there was no need to ever look any further than the kingdom I was discovering within myself and now knew lay deep within every human being.

Outside of my meditations, when I was in activity, my complete physiology was slowing down to an incredibly calm, serene, unflappable state of being. My mind was totally quiet, almost without a thought, but at the same time more alert and awake than it had ever been before. There seemed to be some kind of deep, silent understanding growing within me, a certain type of profound intuitive "knowingness" and my every word, every thought, every action, was charged with that energy, that clarity and that purpose. Suddenly the entire world was brand new to me and I was basking in the pure joy of silent being.

Walking the grounds of campus between meditations, becoming part of that supreme silence I was so dramatically experiencing during my meditations, I also began to notice subtle changes in everything about me. Suddenly everything seemed more alive, more vibrant and conscious than I had noticed before. It was if the entire environment was awake and alert, waiting and watching. And with my newly heightened levels of perception I sensed a conscious intelligence residing within everything and could hear that intelligence whispering, watching and waiting. In fact, I felt it all about me in the plants, the water and the sky, as well as deep within the song of every bird and every breath of wind that caressed my face. Everything was now connected to create one single, unbordered, unbounded, alert, awake, alive, all encompassing universal awareness.

Ending that first week of intense experience and rapid physiological growth and entering into the second, I now began to feel, both within and without of the meditation process, a sensation of warmth and a tingling at the base of my spine. It was as if a warm, liquid light was being poured into that part of my body and filling me full of energy, light, love, and understanding. Yes, as strange as it must sound, something was definitely entering at the base of my spine, rising up through my spinal column and filling my entire body and mind with even deeper and more profound feelings of peace, happiness and rapture. After a while it began to feel like my entire being was transforming into a channel or medium for receiving this energy. I also began to realize that I was not only receiving this energy, but had the ability to direct it outward.

The energy emanated from my solar plexus, abdomen, and facial area. The arrival of the new light-force was opening me up and shining the same force outward; in fact, it was at that point that another strange thing began to happen: I began to feel the opening of my third eye, that metaphysical space between and approximately one inch above the two physical eyes. I could actually feel those four areas of my body opening up and all of that light energy that was entering into me at the base of my spine escaping, or rather shining out!

And those about me began to notice the difference too. Daily, as I went about my normal interactions with the other members of the ashram, people began to say they noticed a certain glow or radiance coming from me, something far beyond the normal range. I simply could not believe that I, Eric Bullard, from Portland, Oregon, was realizing such lofty heights of awareness so suddenly. What was happening to me was usually reserved for great seers and sages hidden away in remote Himalayan caves, not for young sales executives on a one-month retreat. I was humbled, honored, amazed, and to tell the truth, a little bit scared. Was I ready for all of this? Was I going too fast? Should I really be going this far, was all of this really safe to be experiencing?

But by that time it was too late to turn back. In fact, nothing was further from my mind. The light force I was receiving through the base of my spine had grown to such a degree that I was now completely charmed, overwhelmed and in fact dominated by it. I had become its servant, a willing servant yes, but still a servant. Doors and channels were being thrown open inside of me and the light force was now pleasantly roaring into me and then racing out again through my solar plexus and facial area as still more energy poured into me at the base of my spine. It was an overwhelming flood of rapture, excitement and at the same time deep peace that was racing through me and removing all obstacles and then flowing out again. It simply would not be denied.

That feeling of Sacredness that I had begun to experience during the first week of the course continued to expand and I began to feel on an incredibly deep, intimate, personal level the complete Sacredness of all life, everyone and everything. I realized that this thing that we were all living together, this thing called "life" in all of its variety, suffering, boredom, struggle, sometimes happy, sometimes sad, sometimes good, sometimes bad, was absolutely Sacred on a scale of gigantic proportions. And in realizing that, every single thing, act, very word, now began to be seen and realized as part of the Sacred, hallowed journey of being a human being: Wholeness becoming the fragmentation of human experience and the mistake of the intellect and then the process of fighting, learning, and struggling to get back to that same Wholeness.

It was that sense of "I" as an individual that was the root cause of all of my problems, anxieties, insecurities and fears. That sense of "I" as a separate entity that led to unending desire, feelings of incompleteness and constant inner yearning. But now, due to the amazing transformation that was taking place within me, "I "was transcending the little, individual "I" that "I" had been all of my life and becoming a very connected part of the gigantic Wholeness, Oneness of everything that "I" was experiencing more and more everyday through my meditations.

Sometime around the end of week two I finally admitted to myself that I really was on the threshold of discovering something so incredibly large and fantastic that I dared not try and put a name or definition to it. I didn't really know if it was by accident that I had carelessly stumbled onto this new level of consciousness and experience that I was entering into; but this thing that was happening was big, bigger than big, and no mere everyday experience. Even with more

than six years of serious study and profound experience in the field of meditation, even with over thirteen
years of voracious reading, experience, and study in
affiliated topics, I had never come close to what I was
experiencing now. In fact, I had read about similar
experiences in only the most advanced or extraordi-
nary cases. But the incredible depth, magnitude, and
duration of this thing that was suddenly unfolding
itself to me in such a swift, sure and dramatic manner assured me that it was no joke, no fluke, and no
everyday experience. No, this was something big,
something far beyond mere learning, the intellect, or
human experience, as we generally know it to exist.

4

CHIAPAS, MEXICO, 1998

*The Divine Power, Kundalini, shines like the stem
of a young lotus; like a snake, coiled round upon
herself, she holds her tail in her mouth and lies
resting half asleep at the base of the body.*
YOGA KUNDALINI UPANISHAD (1.82)

I AWAKE TWO weeks later to bright blue skies, exit my
room at the Posada Casa Real, enter the sun-drenched
courtyard, and fall into a labyrinth of activity. Seated
around a table are two young women from Argentina
drinking extremely strong tea out of some kind of tall
silver cup that suspiciously resembles a Persian hookah. Sitting in the corner is a full-blooded Aztec Indian
reading a copy of Homer's Odyssey translated into
Spanish. Out on the terrace, a young Parisian couple

is playing bawdy cabaret tunes; she flails away on a beat up old accordion, Gauloise haphazardly dangling from her lips, and he, in a battered beret, manically switches back and forth between guitar and trumpet.

At the top of the stairs four Germans (or are they Swiss?) are attempting to funnel their bicycles down the stairway and off to the ancient Mayan ruins of Palenque. The radio is turned up full blast and a reporter in rapid fire Spanish is giving the latest details of the five-year-old Zapatista uprising. Today's news; forty-three innocent Indigenous villagers gunned down by a paramilitary group in the hamlet of Acteal one hour north of San Cristobal. *La Señora*, owner of the *posada*, climbs the stairs, weaves her way through the departing cyclists, flips the radio dial until she finds Julio Iglesias and begins washing the day's dirty linen. *Sombrero* perched precariously upon her head, she hums along out of tune with Julio happy in the fact that the *posada* is almost full and money is coming in. Suddenly the front bell rings and she is off to greet more new arrivals.

I shower, shave, take a few sips of *mate* tea from the big silver hookah then descend the stairs and hit the streets of San Cristobal. Once again the streets are packed and Calle Real de Guadalupe is humming with activity for in the two weeks since the Virgin de Guadalupe celebration there has been a steady influx of tourists arriving for the holidays. In fact, it is Christmas Eve day and it appears as if the entire world has descended upon San Cristobal to celebrate. Indians and Nationals from all over Mexico are bartering, trading, visiting, and seeing the sights; mongrel mobs of European hippies in dreadlocks and faded Guatemalan multi-colored clothing search for cheap drugs and the international party scene; *Tzotzil* women, half-running, half-walking dart through the crowd, live chickens in their hands while others are hawking everything from wool *chamarras* to *rebozos* to hand woven belts and bracelets. There are Americans in Levi's and baseball hats, Italians in Gucci's and designer sunglasses, and Germans in group tour formation marching down the sidewalk. There are French tourists, Dutch tourists, and Japanese tourists taking pictures of everything. They're all here clogging the narrow sidewalks and turning San Cristobal into one giant international Christmas party. I slowly work my way through the crowd aiming myself towards the *mercado principal* (large, outdoor market) and breakfast.

After fifteen minutes of swimming my way through the international crowd of partygoers I finally arrive at the *mercado* and direct myself towards my favorite food stall and the cheapest, most flavorful breakfast in San Cristobal. But here the congestion has reached mammoth proportions. It is absolutely insane and totally impassable. Taxis, buses, cars, carts and people all jam the narrow lanes leading into the *mercado* pushing, honking and screaming in unison. I once again slowly and meticulously work my way through the crowd and then finally enter the *mercado* itself only to be assaulted by an even thicker, more impregnated mass of humanity buying, selling, pushing and shoving. It is the ultimate, orgasmic, holiday shopping spree. The entire *mercado*, all eight square blocks, is a whirlwind of breathless activity; fruits of all kinds, vegetables, firewood, live pigs, chickens and turkeys, watches, bootlegged cassettes, flowers, a dozen types of cheese, fish, goats, *chorizo, elotes, ocote*, thrown off recycled Western clothes, *sombreros*, candles and anything and everything else your heart could desire or detest is for sale. Mexican and Indigenous sales-men and women scream, promise and cajole while firecrackers blast off at random intervals amidst the seething, pulsating, near hysterical crowd helping to give the entire mad, rushing scene a feeling some-what similar to that of the Mekong Delta during the Tet offensive.

I shimmy, swerve and shake my way through the mob and then finally find my favorite breakfast stall where I bolt down a tasty meal of *pollo entomatado*. Breakfast finished, I pay my tab and once again try to squeeze my way through the hysterical crowd of beggars, buyers, sellers and thieves. Scones, two for one *peso*, wooden crucifixes, old Spanish coins, plastic Christmas trees and the like are being bought and sold at a maddening pace. I am assaulted from every angle as I twist, turn, dance, and gyrate my way through the mounting rush of traffic and pedestri-ans. Sheep's wool, *mochilas*, mangos five for a dol-lar, framed portraits of the Holy Virgin, Jesus Christ, Jean-Claude Van Damme and Pamela Sue Anderson, fortunetellers, soothsayers, taco stands, snake oil salesmen, jugglers, cripples, stray dogs and brightly colored groups of *Indigenas* all block my path.

Finally after ten minutes, I make my way through the crowd to the Santo Domingo church and market hoping to find a little breathing room. How could I have been so foolish? Once again I find a seething, throbbing, international crowd buying, selling, gawking and haggling with the Indigenous marketers; wooden masks from Tapachula, wool rugs from Oaxacca, amber from the mines of Simojovel and embroidered shirts from San Juan Chamula and Aguacatenango, belts, bags, blankets, baubles, knives, bracelets, anklets and earrings in all shapes, sizes, and colors, tapestries, napkins, tablecloths, shawls, shirts, dolls, pants, shorts, wallets and hats, jade from Honduras, incense from Guatemala, necklaces, arrowheads, turquoise, precious stones and of course *tacos, tostadas, tortas, helados, bolis*, and sweets of all kinds. I quickly size up the entire scene as impossibly hopeless and beat a hasty retreat back to the relative peace and quiet of my hotel.

───◦◦◦───

I reach the hotel around noon and find my newfound German friend Gene stretched out on the terrace, shirtless, sipping a rum and coke and chatting merrily away with a large group of international tourists. At noon he is already draining his third double cocktail. All of us are gathered around the tables with new groups constantly arriving and departing, the excitement of Christmas Eve mixes with that of being in San Cristobal and everyone is jabbering away a mile a minute in a strange mixture of Spanish, English and half a dozen European languages while a growing crescendo of rockets and fireworks explodes out in the street and overhead.

Before I know it I am back out in the street, rushing through the crowd and searching for the nearest store and a bottle of Bacardi rum and some Coca-Cola. Suddenly I am caught up in the largest, most frenzied international Christmas party I have ever seen. Back at the hotel I pour myself a tall rum and coke, greedily gulp it down, and prepare another. The stereo comes out, the volume soars, the Aussies break out a bottle Oaxacan *mescal*, the Israelis open another round of Noche Buena beer, and the Italians leave in search of some good red wine while Gene and I continue mixing rum and cokes underneath the bright blue skies.

By 6:00 PM we are feeling no pain and in fact wholeheartedly continuing with our manic holiday celebrations; the Italians have returned from the market with various bottles of red wine from Chile and are offering full glasses to anyone interested. The Aussies are knocking back shots of *mescal* and chasing them down with ice cold Sol beer. The Israelis are brewing strong coffee to mix with their newly acquired bottle of Kahlua and Gene is doggedly continuing along with double rum and cokes. People arrive, people depart, and bottles are passed and drained while Gene twists up a couple of fat joints which are eagerly shared and approved of by all. Stories are told about travels in Honduras, Costa Rica, India, and the Hindu Kush. The sun begins to set in the west, the stars come out and the fireworks display overhead intensifies. Around 8:00 PM it is decided that dinner and a stroll to the *zocalo* are in order so we temporarily close down the bar, bundle up against the oncoming cold, and depart for dinner.

Leaving as a group, all twelve of us snake our way through the jammed streets of San Cristobal. Skyrockets blast off overhead, firecrackers explode at our feet and a cacophony of car horns, sidewalk stereos, laughter and screams fill the air. After a few short blocks we become lost, then separated in the maddening crowd. A few blocks later we come together again, become lost again, then somehow miraculously find ourselves in front of our planned destination; Las Estrellas restaurant. We secure a table near the back of the restaurant and then settle down for a much deserved and, at this point, much needed Christmas Eve dinner of *enchiladas, tostadas*, pasta, soups, salads and of course more beer. Conversation turns to the evening's entertainment and it is quickly decided that the *zocalo* holds the highest possibility of fun and adventure. Dinner over, the bill paid, we bundle ourselves up once more against the cold and set off into the cold, clear, star-studded evening.

Arriving at the *zocalo* we find it lit up like a Christmas tree and swirling with activity. Small stalls abound selling sweets, hotdogs, hamburgers, popcorn, corn on the cob, coffee and *pox* (a nasty local liquor second only to white lightning in punch and power). Children are playing, couples and entire families are strolling along leisurely hand in hand, and tourists from more than twenty different countries gawk, stare, take pictures and haggle with the Indigenous salespeople. There is even a Mexican Santa Claus ho-ho-ho-ing and tossing candy to a ragged mob of Indigenous street children.

We take it all in then amble over to the square in front of the gigantic central cathedral, dwarfed in size only by the mighty Santo Domingo church complex. Here we find a large, mixed group of over two hundred Mexicans, Indians and international tourists standing in front of a giant screen T.V. watching a newscaster interview the inhabitants of Acteal who are describing the most recent attack there by the paramilitary. Behind the stage Televisa (Mexico's largest television conglomerate) has parked one of their semi-trucks mounted with a huge satellite dish ready to relay the most recent developments in the ongoing war.

We watch the interviews for a while, become bored, then switch back to the *zocalo* where we find a small pick-up band from the state of Oaxaca playing traditional Mexican folk songs. We listen for a short while and watch the dancers before shifting over to the other side of the *zocalo* where five boys from Ecuador are pumping out instrumental numbers from the Andean highlands. Across the packed *zocalo* I notice two military Humvee vehicles, each mounted by a helmeted, grim faced soldier aiming a fifty-caliber machine gun directly into the crowd. In addition, there are about twenty heavily armed soldiers mingling around the vehicles. But my concern and fear quickly turn to smiles as I see at least ten of the soldiers buying Subcomandante Marcos (leader of the opposition Zapatista forces) t-shirts from a crafty Indigenous saleslady. Burnt out on the hyper drive of the *zocalo* we huddle together once again and beat a hasty retreat back to the hotel and our terrace under the stars.

Arriving back at the *posada* we find yet another mixed group of new arrivals huddled around the second floor terrace toasting in Christmas. They greet us with a loud round of cheers and drink invitations, we break out our supplies, and a whole new level of manic conversation, toasts and laughter echoes into the night. Drinks are poured, bottles are drained, and Gene continues rolling and passing around joints of the prime Mexican grade.

Taking a break from the conversation and scene around me I glance up into the evening sky and realize that I can no longer tell the stars from the rockets blasting off overhead. It's been quite a day. But now the drink, the Mexican marijuana, the cold, the sky-rockets and the stars are all starting to blend together and affect me in a strange, pleasant sort of way. Suddenly I feel warm and fuzzy all over, happy to be a million miles away from home with a group of complete strangers drinking, toasting and talking about absolutely nothing relevant. Slowly I bring myself back down to earth, take one last glance around at the maddening party scene, light up another cigarette, put my feet up on the table, and fall into a deep, comfortable, catatonic sleep.

5

THE ASHRAM, 1989

Do not struggle. Go with the flow of things,
and you will find yourself at one with
the mysterious unity of the universe.
CHUANG TZU

THINKING ABOUT ALL that was happening from the point
of view I managed to retain in the face of everything,
I could not help but analyze my amazing awakening.
What could be the cause? In part it was the course
and the extended hours of meditation and yoga
sutras, but other people had done the same for the
same amount of time without such a dramatic awakening. But what about the marma-aroma therapy that
I had begun just before the course? I was sure it had
something to do with what was happening, as well as
the combination of herbs that I was taking in the Amrit
Prash. I wasn't sure what was in the Amrit Prash but I

knew it contained a healthy dose of Ashwaganda as well as Gotu Kola. I knew that Gotu Kola increased blood flow to the brain, so that made sense, but there was something else going on. Could it be that my system was so acutely fragile and sensitive that the strong combination was affecting me more intensely than my fellow students?

I knew that the marma-aroma therapy and the Amrit Prash were both relatively new to the general public and their usage in combination with extended hours of meditation and the yoga sutra program was known to very few Westerners at that time. But still, what was happening to me went far beyond all of that. In fact, it was completely beyond anything I could have imagined. But the way it reassured and delighted me as it unfolded made it so easy to go along with. And the pace continued to accelerate.

By week three of the course my consciousness had transcended the relative plane of existence as we know it. I had broken through, and was breaking through more each day into a new world. This was something I read about in the Hindu texts but not something I thought I would achieve in my lifetime. But now it was actually happening! I was quickly moving up the ladder of consciousness and edging closer and closer each day to a real sense of enlightenment as opposed to the small, passing glimpses that I had been experiencing the last six years.

Each and every day, each and every meditation, I could sense my mind becoming purer and purer and filling with the absolute truth I was contacting through my extended meditations. "Pure" I say because all of the remaining thoughts and ideas in my mind were being absorbed and melted away by the Supreme Silence I was contacting through my meditations. And in the absence of that constant rush and complexity of ongoing thoughts I was transcending coarse sensory input and knowledge and coming into contact with direct experience of the Absolute. Yet it wasn't me doing it. I was a neutral observer of this experience. It was all coming about by the incredible white light that was entering at the base of my spine and completely changing my life.

All remaining boundaries were being swept away now and as the days continued I found myself slowing down more and more and becoming quieter and quieter. I was no longer a thinking, doing human being but a channel for this amazing light force to enter the world. I was humbled, excited, acutely aware of exactly what was going on and energized yet strangely fatigued at the same time. I considered trying to slow the process down, control it a bit, but it was so overwhelming and powerful that I simply couldn't resist its force. I just wanted to keep pushing onward, ever eager to see what miracles the next day would bring. Suddenly everything was becoming so clear, so obvious and so simple. There were no more errors, no more mistakes or coincidences but rather everything happening in one glorious harmony woven together without friction to fulfill a Divine, complete, undeniable will.

Mid-way through week three my vision began to deepen and I began to perceive everything on a molecular level. I could obviously still see the gross level of reality as we know it, but at the same time I began to see the fine molecular structure, the base on which everything in the relative world is founded. Yes, I could actually, visibly see the underlying molecular structure of physical existence and creation, and observe the fact first hand that everything was made up of one singular energy force: that of whirling atoms and molecules. I now had the very clear and direct understanding that the different sizes, shapes, textures, and densities of the physical world were a result of the difference in the vibratory levels or frequencies of that same underlying atomic structure. There were now no more physical boundaries for me, no more separateness! No more empty space between the earth and sky, a tree and a building, me and another person. Everything was one in the same, bending, weaving, pulsating, and flowing to create one eternal, omnipresent river of Divine destiny. And I could also detect a buzz or humming coming from and going through it all; all of those molecules and atoms in motion creating a beautiful song: the song of creation. And still, the pace of my evolution continued to accelerate.

My entire physiology was changing at an astonishing rate due to the light-force that was still rushing into my being through the base of my spine. And with these changes certain powers began to avail themselves to me. Or rather, I was growing, learning, and evolving at such a rate that new levels of awareness, consciousness, intelligence, and ability were becoming part of my everyday experience.

Besides the abilities to give *darshan*, the Hindu concept of shining the light of true knowledge outwards, on a limited basis and perceive the world beyond its physical boundaries, I was now beginning to read minds! I would be listening to someone and they would be going on about this and that and while they were speaking, while I was listening to their normal conversation, I would hear something else; a perception of what they were really feeling, what they really wanted to say. It was almost as if I was hearing two dialogues! Both were real, but what the person was usually expressing verbally often served merely as a smokescreen for their true feelings, while the other more subtle message or communication that I was perceiving on that intuitive or telepathic level contained the real truth. This second, subtler message I was picking up came directly from the soul, or the heart, where their spoken dialogue usually contained nothing more than irrelevant chatter. To the reader this must sound a little farfetched but if you think about it you have probably had the exact same experience, albeit, on a much smaller and simpler level; that of listening to someone and although they are saying one thing to you your "gut" or intuition is hearing a completely different message. It was that exact same experience though on a far greater and deeper scale.

And then a few days after that I began to have the experience of actually being able to read, or rather see someone's past; their experiences, the problems they had faced, and how these things all worked in concert to form their present reality, perception of the world, and more importantly, their possible future. I realized that more often than not we are merely creations of our past, formed today by our mistakes, successes, and experiences of that past. Seeing all of this I also got a rough idea of what the future might hold for this person. But the most fascinating thing for me was to simply sit and listen to someone speak. To hear those two voices, simultaneously, that of the personality chattering away trying to deceive, impress, or manipulate and that subtler voice of the soul which always spoke the clear, direct truth. It fascinated me to see the difference between the two.

6

CHIAPAS, MEXICO, 1999

This Atman shines with its own light. Its power is infinite. It is beyond sense knowledge. It is the source of all experience.
SHANKARA'S CREST JEWEL OF DISCRIMINATION

A WEEK LATER I wake up early and head back down to the *mercado*. Once there I climb into a *colectivo* and squeeze myself into a seat along with the other ten Mexican and Indigenous passengers that are heading south this morning. Though still a bit groggy I am excited beyond words. Today I am off to Guatemala. Guatemala, oh how I know it well! By now I have been visiting and exploring Guatemala for over three years and in that time have become totally enraptured by the country, it's culture, and it's

Indigenous *pueblos* sprinkled throughout the northern highlands. Of course I know the capital, the colonial elegance of Antigua, the majestic beauty of Lago Atitlan and Central America's largest Indigenous market in Chichicastenango. But it is the Cuchamatane Mountains to which I am heading today that have really captured my heart.

Rising to a frosty 10,800 feet above sea level, the Cuchamatane Mountains of Northern Guatemala are the tallest non-volcanic peaks in Central America. The lower levels are richly soiled and cultivated by Indians and *Ladinos* (people of combined European and Native American descent) producing abundant crops of coffee, corn, fruits, and vegetables. Further up, the near-perpendicular slopes turn barren, cold, foggy and rainy, and are scattered with giant boulders, shriveled pines and excellent pasturage for the flocks of sheep that the Indigenous population graze there. Between the peaks, tucked away in the numerous deeply cut valleys scattered throughout the range, hundreds of isolated, traditional Indigenous villages continue living an ancient, agrarian lifestyle thousands of years old and far removed from the modern world. In the 70's and 80's the Cuchamatanes were the scene of bitter fighting between the Guatemalan army and guerrilla forces, but with the signing of the peace accord of the mid-90's, peace and tranquility have finally returned to the Cuchamatanes.

An hour south of San Cristobal I catch another *colectivo* in the town of Comitan and ride a half hour to the crossroads that head east to El Parque Nacional

Los Lagunas de Montebello. I wait there for a few minutes then catch my third *colectivo* of the day to the small village of Lazaro Cardenas. The village is nothing more than a crossroads with a scattering of huts and two small stores, but this is where I have to exit the *colectivo* and wait for a ride to the border thirty minutes away. Usually I take the Pan American highway directly south from San Cristobal and enter Guatemala through La Mesilla. This time I have chosen a new route via the backside of the Cuchamatanes. It is a remote, lesser known route, sparsely populated and totally un-touristed. Not only am I the only *gringo* that climbs into the back of the pickup truck that will ferry us to the border, I'm the only non-Indigenous. The other ten passengers are short, thin, brightly dressed Guatemalan Indians on their way back to their highland villages after a few weeks of illegal work in Mexico.

For half an hour or so we drive along the deeply rutted dirt road past fields of corn, thin forest, and the occasional farmhouse. The pickups' broken muffler and the open-air travel make conversation difficult but somehow we manage to communicate the usual traveler's inquiries as we bounce along towards the border; where are you from, where are you going, and so forth. It is these Indians who keep me coming back to the Cuchamatanes. After three years of travel in the highlands I still find myself fascinated by their culture, their way of life, and their unique perspective on life itself. The people I'm travelling with are from the small village of Yambalajoch, one hour on the other side of the border. All brightly dressed, the women shy, quiet, viewing me suspiciously and always with an assortment of bundles and children, the latest born invariably suckling at their breasts; the men inquisitive, proud, humble, and always carrying a finely sharpened machete.

Arriving at the border we find the Mexican side to be no more than a small, tan colored immigration office with a few chickens strolling about outside. Climbing down out of the truck and paying the driver for my passage I make my way over to the immigration office while the Indians from Yambalajoch silently disappear into the trees. Entering the immigration office I find it manned by two drunken immigration officials in tan and khaki uniforms. Surprised by the sight of a *gringo* they ask where I'm from, where I'm planning to go and explain that I am the first non-*Ladino*, non-Indian to cross the border here in over a year. They go on to say that due to current political circumstances they have no authority to grant me an exit visa from Mexico and that even if they did, they lack the official rubber passport stamp and so it is officially illegal and impossible for me to exit Mexico and enter Guatemala at this crossing. Breaking into hysterical laughter they pour themselves another drink and sit back to watch my response. Five years in Mexico and Guatemala have taught me not to panic in situations like this so I pull out my cigarettes, offer them up, chat for about ten minutes, and then with a wink and a smile they wave me through. I walk the 100 yards to the actual border, cross through a broken gate, and officially arrive in the Republic of Guatemala and the town of Gracias a Dios.

If Gracias a Dios isn't an improvement over the Mexican side of the border at least it's bigger. There are a few small stores scattered along the dusty, treeless main street, a pharmacy, a school, three restaurants, and a couple of broken down hovels that are trying to pass themselves off as hotels. Past "Main Street" I can see a collection of small shanties and even a dozen or so "real houses" so I'm going to guess the population here of mixed *Ladinos* and Indians is somewhere around 2,000. But the town itself has a familiar heaviness to it. It's the dirty, anxious, angry, sad feeling I feel in every border town I have visited in Mexico from Tijuana to Tapachula. Looking around I don't see an immigration office, I don't see any police, I don't even see the usual horde of moneychangers hovering like vultures. In fact, I don't see anyone that I feel like talking to, just blank, hungry stares following me wherever I go.

—— ❄ ——

My first job is to find the Guatemalan immigration office and that should be relatively easy in a small town like this. Wandering around for a bit I finally walk into one of the stores on Main Street to ask and find out it is housed in a small building next to the schoolhouse in the middle of town. I wander over to the schoolhouse, enter the small building next door to it, and introduce myself to the part-time immigration officer, part-time schoolteacher sitting behind the desk half asleep. After a few pleasant inquiries he stamps my passport with a three-month Guatemalan visa, shakes my hand, and officially welcomes me to the Republic of Guatemala. I ask about changing money and the approximate departure time of the next bus heading out of Gracias a Dios towards the Cuchamatanes. Changing money will be no problem, he says. At the pharmacy on Main Street I can buy all of the *quetzales* I want. But getting out of town is another thing, because the last bus out of town today already left. Nope, it looks like I am going to have to spend the night in town and then catch a bus out first thing tomorrow morning.

Suddenly despondent, I pick up my passport and walk to the nearby pharmacy, fearfully noting the blank, hungry, almost criminal stares that follow me down the street. But luck is with me once again as I arrive at the pharmacy to change my *pesos* into *quetzales*. The pharmacist has a friend, a travelling salesman, who is about to leave for the Cuchamatanes, and although he will be making many stops along the way and will only get me half way to my final destination of Todos Santos, I leap at the opportunity to escape from Gracias a Dios. Twenty minutes later I find myself exiting town seated in a brand new Toyota 4X4 complete with stereo and air conditioning.

My new friend's name is Pedro and he is from Guatemala City. He sells pharmaceutical supplies throughout the department (state) of Huehuetenango, the department in which the majority of the

Cuchamatane Mountains lay. Every week he winds his way up and down the mountains and steep valleys visiting the tiny villages and towns on sales calls returning every weekend to his wife and his family in Guatemala's capitol city.

Leaving Gracias a Dios we travel through a barren, uninhabited, desert landscape with the Cuchamatanes looming directly ahead of us in the distance. Our conversation is as sparse as the country we are travelling through so I gaze out the window and marvel at the desolate wilderness surrounding us. After an hour or so we enter the foothills of the Cuchamatanes where we begin to see trees and signs of life again. We drive down into a forested bowl with a clear running stream and suddenly run smack dab into the annual *fiesta* of the small Indigenous *pueblo* of Nenton. Bam, welcome to Guatemala! The normally sleepy hollow is packed with Indians in their brilliantly colored dress. There are food stands, partygoers, music, drunks, dogs, pigs, a dilapidated Ferris wheel, and the most desperate traffic jam I have ever seen. It is overflowing, manic, and quite a different reality than the barren desert we have just crossed.

Slowly but surely we battle our way over the one lane bridge leading into town and squeeze our way through even narrower streets until Pedro finds a parking space and sets off on business promising to return in an hour or so. I eagerly exit the pickup and set off to wander the streets, take in the sights, and enjoy the party. And what a party it is! All year long these Indians work and save and sweat and toil for these four short days in January when they all come into town, get drunk, spend all of their money, dance, fight, buy novelties and household items for the coming year, and then make their way back to their homes in the surrounding mountains.

I am definitely back in Guatemala now. Everyone is so much shorter, so much thinner and so much more malnourished looking than in Mexico. The streets are also dirtier, the dogs scrawnier, the prices so much cheaper, and there is an overall feeling of travelling back in time to the nineteenth century. I buy a neon striped, hand loomed blanket, eat some tacos, try to converse with the Indians, dodge the firecrackers and end up sitting in a store close to where we parked the truck drinking a few Gallo beers.

After an hour or so Pedro returns and we are off again, slowly weaving our way onward and upward through the foothills of the Cuchamatanes. After ninety minutes of travel we come to the isolated *pueblo* of San Antonio Huista where Pedro parks the truck and disappears for another hour or so on business. Leaving San Antonio Huista we climb up through an even steeper set of hills before arriving in the *pueblo* of Santa Ana Huista where Pedro again disappears for an hour leaving me alone in the truck to contemplate life in these remote outposts of civilization. Two hours later we arrive at the halfway point between Gracias a Dios and Todos Santos, a *pueblo* called Jacaltenango.

Now high in the foothills, with evening and a sharp chill in the air, Pedro decides to spend the night. After a brief attempt at hitchhiking to the next town, I join him at Jacaltenango's only hotel. We pay five US dollars for a shared room and another three dollars for an excellent chicken dinner, complete with locally grown coffee and handmade tortillas. Afterwards, I take a short walk to see the town, have a few beers outside one of the stores while talking with the local Jacal Indians, eat a bag of popcorn and then thank you and goodnight.

7

THE ASHRAM, 1989

*To see a World in a grain of sand and Heaven
in a wild flower, to hold Infinity in the palm
of your hand, And Eternity in an hour.*
WILLIAM BLAKE

ALMOST DRUG-LIKE NOW in its manifestation and intensity, I was constantly amazed by the experience unfolding within me and around me. But it unfolded in such a rational, logical, and completely understandable way that it was impossible to deny its validity. This was not an artificially induced high. This was the normal functioning of the human brain freed from superficial constraint. Read any number of books on meditation, Kundalini, the chakras, or the Yoga Sutras of Patanjali and you will find all kinds of stories, documented experiences, and techniques that will uphold and articulate this entirely possible, yet rare phenomenon.

Books at this time became an interesting experience for me for with my new abilities of perception I was able to lay my hand upon any book cover and read or rather absorb the spirit of the book and even some of its finer points. I distinctly remember walking the aisles of the campus library, going from book to book, laying my hand on each cover, and getting a pretty good idea of what was inside; this book being about a world war, full of sadness, violence and pain, written by a pained author trying to understand the outrages committed against his people; that book written by a caring physician about helping terminally ill cancer patients.

I began to realize that, as modern science says, we really are using only a fraction of our brains' full potential. For from when we are born until our twenties we learn, grow, and mentally develop at a slow, steady rate then sometime during our twenties that rate decreases until we reach a point of arrested development. Most people reach a peak experience of development in their twenties or early thirties with a possible eight to twelve percent (I think it is a lot less) actualization or development of the brains total capacity, geniuses a little more. But now, due to all that was happening on the course, I felt I had tapped a unique opportunity to go way beyond that expected norm.

I have no metric to quantify the progress I made, but I am certain my experiences were concrete examples of what a normal human being's brain was capable of when allowed to develop beyond "normal" standards. And so these things that were happening, these "miracles" that were occurring in my life and becoming a part of my everyday experience were not magic or voodoo; nor were they the hallucinations of some madman or drugged-out teenager. No, this was the heightened reality that resulted when one was allowed to develop to his or her fullest potential. And the pace of development was still increasing daily.

Walking around campus the natural world was now constantly whispering to me. The trees, the flowers, the grass, the sky, and the very air itself were actually singing aloud the joy of creation, and it was more beautiful than anything I had ever seen or heard in my life. Walking past the small lake on campus one day I suddenly had an undeniable urge to try and walk across its surface. What? Walk across the surface of the lake like Jesus Christ? How absurd! But when I thought about it I realized Jesus Christ was a human being too but it was his direct knowledge, direct experience of God, and the realized Kundalini within himself that allowed him to live a higher reality, transcend the physical laws of the universe as we know them, and perform so called miracles. And so after a few days of contemplation on the subject I began to understand how Jesus Christ was able to walk on water, feed thousands, and heal with his hands.

It felt as if I were reaching a divine level of consciousness through the amazing force that was entering the base of my spine and filling my mind and body. I truly felt as if I had stumbled upon and was on the very edge of the greatest discovery of all time. In fact, I felt as if I was a breath away from something so fantastic and unimaginable that I couldn't have stopped myself even if I wanted to. So I decided to trust what was happening. Trust 100 percent and let go. I decided to open myself completely and surrender to that force that was so dramatically entering into and changing my life. And in doing so I believed I would attain the highest goal of mankind: total enlightenment.

Moving into week four of the course was like entering into pure Divinity itself as the past and future dissolved into the concentrated and powerfully serene rapture of the present moment of pure being. I could still remember the past or project my mind into the future if I wished, but why? It wasn't reality in any sense of the word any more. And anything that was there would definitely be dwarfed by the majesty of being right now. In fact, I could feel my past and future resolving and collapsing into that same now. No past, no future, no ruminations of that past or need to make plans for the future or even something minutes away. The future was simply unfolding itself right now naturally and harmoniously minute by minute, second by second in perfect correlation with natural law and preordained destiny.

And then the course ended. Boom, just like that. I mean, I knew it was going to end. I was somewhat prepared for an ending. But what was I going to do now? After this, how was I going live a life as a sales executive back in Portland, Oregon? Way too much had happened. But at the same time, things couldn't keep going as they had been going for the past thirty days because I had major commitments back home. I had a life there; home, career, relationships, and debt. I had to go home and get back to work! Christmas was coming up. Major sales trips were in the works. There was a West Coast book convention in October. People were depending on me. I had to go back to my life and function in the material world.

When the course ended I also began to wonder if I was actually ready to see and experience all that I had seen and experienced. I had done the course and all of the Ayurvedic therapies just as I had been instructed but I suspected I had too gone deep, too quickly. Had I pushed the envelope beyond my human abilities of comprehension? Don't get me wrong, it was amazing. But was I ready for all of this? I wasn't sure.

I took a few days there on campus, returned to my regular meditation-sutra program, but kept taking the herbs and practicing the marma aroma therapy program. As I expected, the incredibly giant experience diminished and I returned to a much less heightened and almost "normal" state of consciousness. But I definitely did not feel the same at all and began to realize on some level that things would never be the same again. Something very big had shifted in me and I still recalled everything that transpired on the course and the vivid memories were accompanied by a rising confusion. I had many questions that I needed answered. But the world of time, money and material commitment was waiting so I reluctantly packed my bag and headed to the airport with that now seemingly strange feeling of light energy still entering at the base of my spine.

8

Cuchamatane Mountains, Guatemala, 1999

A flaming serpent rose released from sleep.
It rose billowing its coils and stood erect
climbing mightily, stormily on its way.
SAVITRI, BOOK VII, CANTO 5

WAKING UP THE next morning I have a quick breakfast, bid farewell to Pedro, and catch the early morning bus off to Todos Santos. Eagerly hopping aboard I squeeze into one of the last vacant seats between an Indigenous lady and a drunken *Mestizo* now fast asleep. The driver waits another twenty minutes until the bus is filled beyond capacity, guns the engine until it sounds like it is going to explode, cranks up the volume on his new Rumba Romantica cassette tape to ear splitting volume, grinds the gears until I can see smoke coming out of the engine casing, and we are off.

The Guatemalan bus system and Guatemalan buses in general have never ceased to amaze me; recycled United States Bluebird school buses originally designed to ferry complacent adolescents to and from suburban centers of education, their rebirth in Guatemala is a quaint if not drastic contrast. They are gaudily repainted inside and out, complete with Christmas lights, pictures of girlfriends, mothers, Jesus Christ and the Virgin of Guadalupe hanging over the dashboard, always containing a super blaster sound-system with blown out speakers churning out the latest salsa or cumbia music at ten-plus airport runway volume. Dusty, dirty, smelly, full of garbage and lead laced exhaust fumes, the driver and ticket seller as well as a good percentage of the male passengers are often drunk or well on their way. Forever filled to the bursting point, three, four or five people are crammed into a bench seat originally designed to accommodate two pre-teen youngsters while the center aisle is completely impassable and another dozen or so people are packed onto the roof. Never on time, always late, stopping every 100 yards at every fork in the road or broken down hut, travelling some of the worst roads in the world, prone to breakdowns, flat tires, and overheating, a journey through the Guatemalan highlands on one of these buses is an unforgettable experience and one which is meant to be lived again and again in order to savor the full richness of its cultural textures.

Slowly but surely we weave our way out of town and up a narrow one-lane dirt road dodging oncoming trucks and errant sheep as we head further into the Cuchamatanes. Every five minutes or so the bus grinds to a halt and we pick up or deposit another group of smiling, chattering Indians. The scenery is fantastic for by now we have left the foothills and are making our way up one of the narrow valleys that cuts deep into the heart of the Cuchamatanes. Down to the left lies the valley floor and a meandering stream that becomes smaller as we ascend. To our direct right, and all but scraping the paint off that side of the bus, is the continuing mountainside going up seemingly forever and disappearing into a thick bank of clouds. Almost immediately the majority of the passengers lean their heads forward and fall fast asleep until, as if by some kind of miracle, they magically open their eyes in time for their stop, gather their bags, parcels, farm animals and children, descend off the bus and then trudge off smiling up some muddy track towards home. After almost one and a half hours of constant vertical movement we level out a bit and see the first village of the day ahead.

Concepcion is another small village of about 2,000 souls but it is here for the first time that we begin to see the distinctive costume of the Todos Santos Indigenous, a few mingling in the crowded street. The men wear red and white candy cane striped pants with blue, knee-length overpants and a homespun multi-colored shirt with the biggest, brightest collar available in Guatemala while the women wear a deep blue, ankle-length *corte* (dress) wrapped around the waist and fastened with a bright red *faja* (sash). The main items of interest though are the *huipiles* (intricately patterned, brightly colored, blouses) that the women wear which take 3-4 months of labor to produce.

Arriving in the *zocalo* of this small *pueblo* we are immediately assaulted by hordes of vendors selling everything from *tacos* and bottled water to sandwiches and *sabritas*. They are reaching up to the windows from below and trying to squeeze down the aisle passing out food, making change, and gossiping with friends and relatives. After a short chaotic wait of departures, arrivals, lowering of cargo and adding of new cargo, we blast off again in another cloud of exhaust fumes, salsa music, and grinding gears.

Higher and higher we climb up the canyon side, dwarfed by the immensity of the chasm we are entering, while steeper and steeper becomes the rough road as the bus wheezes and whines its way up the mountain. A half-hour later we leave the world behind and enter into a phantom reality of thick fog, wandering clouds, desolate pines, and mist. Almost all of the passengers are asleep again, the music is momentarily turned off, and a deep silence reigns as I look out the window and wonder at the beauty of it all. As difficult as it is, as dirty, cold, remote, dangerous and inhospitable as it is, I always seem to capture a feeling of deep contentment here in a bus full of silent, sleeping

Indians, floating through the clouds on a quiet, misty day in the remote mountains of Guatemala.

—— ∞∞∞ ——

An hour later we pull into our second stop of the day: San Martin, one hour short of Todos Santos. It is practically a carbon copy of Concepcion: main square, antique church, some small stores, and a lot of adobe huts. We are once again inundated by vendors and new arrivals and the bus is now far beyond capacity, but no one complains. On the contrary, "the more the merrier" seems to be the Guatemalan bus system's Golden Rule. Five minutes of frenzied activity once again and we blast off up the road, ever onward and upward. With each passing mile we see more and more of the Todos Santeros readily identifiable in their traditional dress, herding sheep, carrying firewood or just standing by the side of the road waving at the bus as it passes. Coming close to the 8,000-foot elevation mark now, the weather is becoming quite cold so windows are closed tight, sweaters are brought out, and cold hands are thrust into pockets. And finally up ahead, through the clouds, I spot the village of Todos Santos.

Todos Santos de Las Cuchamatanes, my home away from home and all-time favorite place in the world! We have arrived at last! For years I have been visiting this friendly oasis of hospitality and peace. The first time was three years ago after meeting a girl at the La Mesilla border crossing who raved about it's

people, it's quaintness, it's friendliness and it's unique-
ness. In six months of travel through Central America
she had never met friendlier people or seen prettier
countryside. I arrived the next day, the day before
Christmas Eve, and it was one of the best times of my
entire life.

Rooming with a local Indigenous family, I was in
heaven for those six days as they welcomed me like a
long lost son, housed me, fed me, took me hiking in
the hills, showed me how to bathe in the traditional
chu (sauna), and watched (trying not to laugh) as I
attempted to help with the farm chores. Since then
I have tried to make it back every three months or
so to stay with the same family, sometimes staying
for weeks or even months on end. This was the place
where I could forget my own past, forget the crazy
modern day world, and just be happy in the midst of
the friendliest people I had ever met.

Todos Santos de Las Cuchamatanes was first made
known to the outside world in 1951 by Maud Oakes in
her work, "The Two Crosses of Todos Santos." After
that the dirt road was brought down the valley, a sprin-
kling of tourists began to arrive, a small hotel went up
and a restaurant opened, but almost fifty years later
the town still retains a certain untouristed, undiscov-
ered, simple, homey feel to it. Over the years a few
more hotels have come and gone, a few more restaurants have opened up and the tourists have continued
to arrive, but never more than a handful on any given
day and never enough to change this picturesque village of traditional Mam Indians.

In the early 1980's the mounting Guatemalan Civil War that had been festering in the Cuchamatanes and throughout the country finally came to show its ugly face in Todos Santos. One tragic March evening in 1982 twin forces of the Guatemalan army sealed off the roads and closed in on Todos Santos hoping to catch guerrilla forces that had already fled into the hills. Entering into Todos Santos they immediately began a house-to-house search for hidden guerrillas, collaborators, and caches of arms. Finding nothing they herded all of the men into the church and began to interrogate and torture them, eventually strangling fourteen to death, while a second unit of soldiers went through town setting more than one hundred houses and farms on fire. It was a night of terror most Todos Santeros would prefer to forget but is commemorated by the two crosses erected in the ruins above town.

Winding up the steep streets and into the *zocalo* the bus is immediately surrounded by a horde of village children looking for tourists (I am the only one on this bus) or strangers in need of a night's lodging. Right away I spot Chavela, the oldest daughter of my friends Polo and Nicolasa Mendoza. "Eric, you've arrived," she squeals with delight. "My father is up at the house sewing and my mother is making beef soup," she shouts amidst the pandemonium of passengers fighting their way off the bus while others pass luggage and farm animals down from the roof. Chavela has just completed her twelfth year but already she is a little lady dressed in her blue *corte* and startling beautiful *huipile*. Only twelve years old she is already well-versed in all the work needed to keep a large family going; she can cook, take care of the younger children and farm animals, clean house, wash clothes, weave on a backstrap loom, chop wood and make tortillas by hand. I grab my bag, assure her that I will be right along and head for one of the *cantinas* scattered along the street and a Gallo beer.

Standing in front of the half open window that serves as the bar I order my beer, take a few sips, sit back, and gaze up at the almost perpendicular canyon walls that rise another 2,000 feet to the plateau above. I greedily gulp down my beer, fire up a cigarette, and buy two more beers. Shouldering my pack and sticking the two Gallos in my back pockets I start up one of the streets to the Mendoza house. It's a short, steep climb but I am so incredibly happy that I feel as if I am floating up the mountain.

Passing the hotel-restaurant Casa Familiar I wave to my friend Carolina. "Hello Eric, where have you been? We thought that you had forgotten us," she says. "Oh no Carolina," I assure her. "I was just busy in Mexico, but now I am here and so glad to see you." She wants to engage me in conversation, but the thrill of being here carries me up the hill, so I simply ask about her mother and keep walking with a promise to return tomorrow to catch up on all the village gossip.

Further up the hill I pass Don Concepcion's store and engage in another brief conversation with him. Continuing on I am greeted by children so numerous that I have to strain to remember their names. Next I pass Don Bernardo's store where he also yells out,

"Eric, where have you been? So long since we have seen you, we thought that you had gotten another new girlfriend in Mexico who wouldn't let you out of the house." I smile, wave, and laugh, again promising to return shortly.

Finally I arrive at the Mendoza house, go around to the back yard, and see my friend Polo Mendoza in his usual spot; sitting on the backbench at his sewing machine making candy cane striped pants for the tourists. He looks at me startled for a moment then breaks into a big grin. "Eric you have arrived, it's been so long! Where have you been?" His wife Nicolasa comes out of the kitchen wiping her hands on her apron with the youngest of the Mendoza clan strapped to her back. "Eric, you've finally arrived!" she says. More Mendoza children wander out from the kitchen, they now number nine. Don Lazaro, Polo's uncle, walks over from next door, bible in hand. I present Polo with a beer, open mine, we toast, and he invites me to sit next to him. Suddenly, at least for the moment, I am the happiest man in the entire world.

9

PORTLAND, OREGON, 1989

Not even a shadow of the thought of victory should cross your mind, when with the inner changes wrought, the coiled-up power starts to unwind.
GOPI KRISHA

AFTER A VERY long flight I finally arrived in Portland, Oregon. I was at that point, to a degree, still receiving the same sensation of light entering my body at the base of my spine. I also still felt confused about everything that had happened on the course. I mean, some really big changes had just happened in my life! I had just journeyed to another, very distinct reality and had lived in that reality and profoundly expanded range of experience and perspective for four weeks.

Four gigantic weeks that had had an incredibly large impact on my life, point of view, belief system, and physiology.

Now with my return to Portland and my job I suddenly felt so lost, tired, confused, and uncertain about it all. It was almost as if I were living in some sort of mixed up, dreamy state of non-reality located somewhere between my old life and the new life that I was still experiencing to a large degree. I really needed some time to rest and to just sort out all of the experiences of the last few months. But it was the Christmas season and the workload was heavy so it was easy for me to forget my confusion and throw myself into a busy travel schedule: Northern California during the end of September, then off to Southern Oregon in early October. The second part of October I had meetings and sales calls on the coast before I was off to Eastern Oregon and Idaho.

Mountain Home, Idaho is a small town one hour east of Boise. I remember arriving there sometime in November totally burnt out. My course had finished two months earlier, I had been working ever since and I was still receiving the same strange sensation of light entering my body through the base of my spine and exiting through my solar plexus and facial area. I had no idea what was going on and felt myself becoming more confused and fatigued as the days went by. I unsuccessfully tried to apply reason to my situation, think it over as best as I could, fit the new experiences on the course into my old pattern of thinking but it just wasn't working. Something was wrong, very wrong. I could not go back to living the life that I had known before the course.

I remember arriving in Mountain Home sometime around six in the evening, getting a hotel room and walking a few blocks to a local supermarket to buy something for dinner. Entering the store I remember thinking how big everything seemed; all that open space, the high ceilings and the never-ending aisles of food and products. Suddenly I felt faint, dizzy, and tried to remember what town I was in but my mind drew a complete blank. Then I thought for a moment and tried to remember what state I was in. Again I drew a total blank. I couldn't even remember what state I was in! My mind was a blank slate and try as I could I just could not put my thinking process together enough to figure out where I was in the world. Suddenly complete fear seized me as I turned, rushed out of the store, and raced down dark streets looking for a hotel that I could not even remember arriving at a mere half-hour earlier.

Somehow I managed to find my hotel that night. After a half-hour or so of wandering the dark streets I recognized my pick-up truck parked in one of the hotel parking lots. Back in my room I sat on the edge of the bed where I tried to consolidate my racing thoughts and calm myself down. Just what the hell was going on? Why was I so lightheaded? Why couldn't I remember anything? Something very strange was going on but for the life of me I couldn't figure out what. Finally I went out to my truck and got out the map. With the map spread out before me on the bed, I remembered that I was in the state of Idaho, in a little town called Mountain Home. I sat there for hours afterwards trying to make sense of it all but I was so lightheaded, so unable to focus my thoughts, that after a few hours of fragmented reflection and confusion I just put myself to bed for a restless night of sleep.

I awoke the next day exhausted and still a bit disoriented. I wanted to go home. I needed to go home, see friends, see family, rest and maybe see a doctor too. But I still had four days left on my sales trip. Today I was supposed to visit the resort town of Sun Valley and spend two days there on sales calls. Saturday it was back to Boise and Sunday I would travel back to Portland and try to make sense of all this.

Driving north on Highway 91 through the countryside my fears and doubts slowly began to subside and I began to feel better. Of course I had been a little disoriented last night and who wouldn't have been? I had been traveling so much the last eight weeks anyone in my position could have felt the same thing. And tired? Of course I was tired. I had been working hard the last two months. Yes, thinking about it in the clear light of day it all started to make sense and I began to relax and feel like my old self once again.

Sun Valley, Idaho is a small, picturesque resort town on the edge of the Rocky Mountains that I knew well. As a boy my father had often taken the entire family there skiing in the winter. In the summer he and I would return alone to camp and fish the numerous trout streams in the area. Years later as a young man I moved to Sun Valley and lived and worked there for almost three years. Now, working for the family publishing business, I still made my way back there every four months or so on a sales trip. And this time, like all the others, I was looking forward to the mountain climate and seeing old friends. Arriving around noon on Thursday I made some sales calls and got a hotel for the night. Yes, I was feeling much better now. The strange dizziness and confusion of the day before must have been some sort of fluke, some sort of strange, passing, travel related disorientation. That night I made some phone calls, went out to dinner with some old friends, and got a good night's sleep.

Awakening Friday morning I finished up my sales calls in town and went out for a short walk in a favorite canyon of mine one-half hour north of town. Driving back into town afterwards I decided to go by the restaurant where I used to work and see some friends. Entering the restaurant I took a seat at the counter and ordered lunch. But then, right in the middle of lunch, there it was again; out of nowhere the same lightheadedness, mental confusion and indefinable, vague fear descending upon me. I tried to maintain some sense of balance but I was having an extremely difficult time focusing myself, following the conversation, and communicating with my friends. With great difficulty I was able to finish my meal, say goodbye to my friends, and drive back to my hotel.

Back in my hotel room I sat on the edge of my bed trying to calm myself down and make sense out of what was going on. I had no idea what was causing the strange set of repeating symptoms. Was I working too hard? Was I traveling too much? Was all of this somehow related to the incredibly beautiful experiences that I had three months earlier in the ashram? For the life of me I couldn't figure it out as my heart beat wildly and my body shook uncontrollably. Finally, after a couple of hours I was able to calm myself down a bit. Afterwards I ate a meager, tasteless supper and focused myself on finishing up the business trip and getting back home to Portland in one piece.

10

TODOS SANTOS, GUATEMALA, 1999

One often reads about the dangers of Kundalini and Kundalini Yoga. These things really are dangerous and not meant to be meddled with in our typically Western way. It is meddling with a fate that strikes the very roots of human existence and can let loose a flood of sufferings that a sane person would never dream possible.
CARL JUNG

SITTING ON THE bench in the back yard of the Mendoza house in Todos Santos with Polo, we launch into a flurry of conversation, Nicolasa joining in from the side. All the new family and Todos Santos gossip and all of my recent travels and activities in Mexico are discussed at lightning speed. Our first beers are quickly drained in all of the excitement so putting the conversation on hold I run up the street to the nearest store for more beer and a pack of cigarettes. Actually it's more of a *cantina* then a store, the only *cantina* this high on the mountain, but they stock a few bags of chips and sell candles in the hope of raising its status from mere *cantina* to that of a store. The three Indians passed out dead drunk in the street though, as well as the half dozen standing around downing Gallo beers and Quetzalteca (Guatemalan white lightning), confirm the fact that this is indeed an establishment where alcohol can be procured.

Stepping over the drunks sprawled out in the street and wading my way through the others that are quickly and diligently trying to reach the same state of intoxication, I approach the front window that serves as a bar and bang my hand on the frame numerous times, calling to those inside the house behind. No one answers so I do it again and again until five minutes later a short Indigenous woman in traditional dress emerges from the back to greet me. "Eric, you have finally come back, where have you been for so long?" It's Doña Angelina, another friend of mine and owner of the store. I order eight beers and some cigarettes, chat with her for a couple of minutes, politely refuse the numerous drink offers from the Indians getting drunk in front of the store, and head back to Polo's house.

Back in the Mendoza's yard I pop open two of the Gallos, pass one to Polo and take my seat next to him on the bench. It feels so good to be here again. In a world that is constantly changing and racing away at a breakaway pace it's nice to know that there is one thing I can always count on; sitting right here with Polo Mendoza, drinking a few beers, and talking away through the afternoon and into the night. Anita, I don't exactly remember where she fits into the Mendoza food chain, crawls into my lap and starts chattering away in a voice that strangely resembles Alvin the Chipmunk. Anita must be about five years old by now, the first time I came up here three years ago she was only two years old and the youngest of the Mendoza children but since then Nicolasa has popped out two or three more Mendozas.

It's actually difficult to remember all of these Mendoza children and their running order. Let's see, Benito is the oldest. He is about nineteen and off in the United States working illegally, sending home money on a monthly basis. Next is Segovia, sixteen, in school part-time, working in the fields part-time. After Segovia follows Chavela, then Jaime, Cristina, Anita, Polo Junior, and Miguel. I don't even know the name of the newest one yet. They're all here except Benito and it really makes for a festive and happy atmosphere; sitting with Polo on the bench, Nicolasa in the kitchen tending the fire and preparing dinner, all the kids, chickens, dogs and cats running in and out of the house making noise while numerous neighbors pass by or come over to sit and visit for a while.

Then there's the *molina* (mill). Two years ago Polo decided to supplement the income he already had coming in from his farm, tailor shop, clothes store and small coffee plantation (nine children create a rather high overhead), so he built a small shack in back of the yard where he grinds corn for his neighbors which they use to make their tortillas. Every day, all day in fact, every fifteen minutes or so, one of the neighbor girls arrives with a basket balanced on her head full of corn grains ready to be ground. They patiently wait at the *molina* door until two or three others arrive and Polo decides that there is enough commerce to warrant his abandoning the sewing machine and cranking up the motor that runs the *molina*. It makes an incredible racket that pierces the stillness of the afternoon but it is more than compensated for by the steady parade of slim, young, stately Indigenous girls that arrive to grind corn for their evening's tortillas. A half hour later as darkness and a cold, clear, crisp evening is descending, Nicolasa emerges from the kitchen and announces that dinner is ready. All eleven of us squeeze into the kitchen and take places around the fire as she passes out bowls of hearty beef soup and thick, handmade Guatemalan tortillas.

The Mendoza house is probably close to 100 years old and made of adobe. It consists of two small rooms with a bare earth floor. It is small and difficult to maneuver in with all of us packed into the kitchen, but it is warm and cozy with a fire burning brightly and night descending. During dinner two other guests arrive who have been staying with the Mendozas the last few days. Anna and Ron are brother and sister, both in their mid-twenties and from Holland. They have been traveling through

Guatemala and Southern Mexico for the last three months and are in Todos Santos for a week or two of hiking and Spanish lessons. The three of us will be sleeping out back in the shed that Polo converted into a guesthouse. We make some room for them, two chairs are brought, Nicolasa dishes them out some soup and they begin their dinner as the rest of us are finishing. His dinner done, Polo burps loudly, announces he still has work to do, and heads back out to the sewing machine.

Finishing my own dinner I give my plate to Nicolasa, crack open another beer and begin talking with Anna and Ron. They seem like good people to me so I contemplate asking them to join me on a hike I will be starting in a couple of days. For almost two years now I have been planning a hike from Todos Santos across the Cuchamatanes to a town on the other side of the range called Nebaj in an area known as the Ixil Triangle. On the map it looks to be a two or three day hike through some of the roughest and least known mountains in Guatemala. The map also shows a secondary road part of the way but I can't be too sure about that. What I am sure of is that I don't want to do the hike alone. I ask Anna and Ron if they'd be interested in joining me. They look at each other for a short moment and agree that it's just the sort of adventure for which they have been looking. We make plans to start sometime after the weekend and then I excuse myself to join Polo on the backbench at the sewing machine.

The sky is pitch black and studded with stars when I go outside. Polo notes that we are out of beer so I make another quick trip up to Doña Angelina's and rejoin him. It's amazing how content I can be just sitting with this man, on this bench, talking away and watching him sew beneath the stars. Every fifteen minutes or so I get up to service the last customers of the day at the *molina*, more neighbors stop by to chat for a while, and everything has a slow, easy, homey and comfortable pace to it. By 8:30 PM, Polo has finally finished his last pair of pants for the day and Ron and Anna have joined us for a few beers. We talk for a while and then they say goodnight and go off to bed early using the fact that tomorrow is market day as an excuse. Polo though, now that his work is done, is ready to party and so at his constant urgings I decide to accompany him down to Main Street and one of the late-night *cantinas*.

By now we've both consumed well over a six-pack of beer each and though Polo is starting to show signs of inebriation, I still feel fresh and invigorated due to the brisk mountain air and the excitement of my arrival in Todos Santos. Leaving the house we wander down the darkened streets, past barking dogs and slowly make our way down to the main street, which at 9:00 PM is still showing signs of life. Walking along Main Street we see that three *cantinas* are still open and doing a lively business. There are also groups of kids running around, people selling food from small stands, and a fair amount of people setting up their stalls to get a head start on the once-a-week market that will begin early tomorrow morning.

We pass by the first two *cantinas* and continue up the street towards the last one where most of Polo's friends like to gather. Like the others, this *cantina* is no more than a store front with an open window through which the owners of the establishment dispatch Gallo beer and Quetzalteca to the small crowd of Todos Santeros gathered around outside. Elbowing our way into the crowd and up to the window we are both greeted as long lost friends and beers are bought for both of us. It's an interesting scene to say the least: 8,000 feet high in the Southern Sierra Mountains of Guatemala, three hours away from anything that even vaguely resembles a real town on a cold, clear, star-studded night, huddled around a dilapidated building with a group of men dressed like circus clowns. All of them are jabbering away a mile a minute in a language I cannot understand even when I am sober. All of us are pounding down "Rooster" beer and white lightning in liver numbing quantities, all the while spitting, swearing, laughing, and smoking Casino cigarettes as fast and furiously as we can inhale them. Yes, an interesting situation to say the least. I must admit though, I do feel at home and in good company here.

And then the crying starts. I have no idea why but, every time these guys get together and start drinking they all start crying and wailing away in a high-strung singsong voice as they loop arms and sway back and forth. It's a complete mystery to me and complicated by the fact that I cannot understand their language. Of course they all speak Spanish and a few even speak pretty good English, but at this point, unless they are speaking directly to me, they all converse in their native tongue. After about twenty minutes or so of crying and swaying, during which time I play the role of passive observer, someone gets upset about something and a fight breaks out. The two combatants are quickly moved away from the window and out into the street where they begin a brawl mainly consisting of threats and half-thrown punches.

Come midnight Polo is incredibly drunk and happily crying away. I am also feeling the effects of the dozen or so beers I have consumed. Buying two more for the road, I tear him from the arms of a friend, we break away from the dwindling crowd, and slowly stagger arm-in-arm up the steep streets to the Mendoza house. Arriving at the Mendoza house Polo goes to bed but I am not ready to sleep, the stars too bright and numerous on this moonless night. Instead, I walk over to the shed and climb the ladder to the roof where I sit beneath the Milky Way, relax and take a few minutes of quiet reflection.

I'm an alcoholic and I know it but I don't care. This is what works: drinking, traveling, always on the road, living with the Indians, and being in the mountains. I never drink in the morning and I'm rarely an everyday drinker. But four, five, sometimes six times a week I get as drunk as I can to forget, to block out all that happened back in the ashram. It's the only thing that works so that's what I do. I was raised a Christian, studied the Bible, went to church and all of that. Heaven for good people, Hell for bad and so on, but nothing I read in any book could have prepared me for what I experienced back there. My God this couldn't be my life, this couldn't be real, but it was and still is. And no matter where I go, no matter what I do, I can never shake the magnitude of that experience.

The pressure I feel, the level of stress that comes from living with this, the memories and constant vigilance are really too much. And then there's the trying to figure it all out. Why did this happen? What does this mean? Does it mean that I have some important spiritual job to accomplish here before my death? I can't tell you how many nights, hours, days, years I have sat and watched this thing reel around and whirl away in my head uncontrollably over and over again. And I keep asking why? But no answers really come so I drink; I drink to maintain some sort of distance and perspective; and I travel or stay in the mountains with the Indians where I seem to fit into their culture and mental-framework.

That cute, quaint, safe life I knew before, that system of beliefs does not exist for me anymore, not after what I experienced back in the ashram. And neither does my ability to be enclosed within the restraints of a city, a full-time job or a normal way of life (by American standards, at least). So I have become an outcast, a wanderer, a bum, a loser and the world's biggest liar constantly questioning not only what happened in the ashram, but also what happened before and everything that is still happening every day.

Another star sparks up and streaks across the sky bringing my gaze and thoughts back to the heavens. My God what a beautiful night, the beauty, the greatness, the grandeur of it all! If God can make and rule all of this, if God is so great and the supreme master of all, why is it accompanied by this incredible suffering? Bringing my gaze back down to earth I polish off the first of my beers, open another, light a cigarette and decide to forget it all for now. For now I'm in the mountains, far away from it all, with the Indians in a small, forgotten *pueblo* that resembles something from 200 years ago. Most important, I'm drunk and beyond the reach of the demons that have hunted and haunted me now for almost ten years.

11

Sun Valley, Idaho, 1989

*Caution is advised for he who lights the eternal
flame of the Sleeping Serpent power known
as Kundalini. And woe is he who awakens
the sleeping dragon without full knowledge to be its master. For it is not quickly
nor with little effort that one burns away
brightly into the sacred flames of Eternity.*
The Sacred Sign of the Snake 3:27

I awoke the next morning feeling a little bit better and
drove the three hours back to Boise where I made
some sales calls before sequestering myself in the hotel. There was still a growing, inescapable feeling of
anxiety, tension, confusion, and panic growing within
me that I could barely control. Could I handle this and

get back to Portland and see a doctor? I had no idea. The situation was deteriorating as the hours went by. Sunday morning I woke up feeling a little better after a full-night's worth of sleep and I hoped that somehow, now that my work was over and I was on my way back to my apartment in Portland, that everything would be all right. I couldn't have been more wrong.

Boise, Idaho to Portland, Oregon is approximately 450 miles. With each passing mile I could feel the symptoms increasing, expanding and becoming more difficult to endure. It was if all the blood in my body was rushing up to my head and filling it beyond capacity, erasing all ability to think, reason or remember. And I could feel it not only in my head but in my eyes, my third eye, and my solar plexus too. The exact same areas where a little over three months earlier I had felt so much light and love!

To what little rational mind I still had left it all seemed so ridiculous. This couldn't be happening, I remember thinking. Not something as strange as this, not so out of the blue, not to me, not right now, not in my life. But it was! It was taking control of my body and mind at an alarming rate and intensity. And worse yet, I still felt totally helpless and in the dark as to what I should do, what I could do to stop it, control it. Stop it, control it? I didn't have the slightest clue what was going on. How was I supposed to confront and stop something I couldn't identify or understand?

Back in my apartment late Sunday night my only desire was to lock the door and hide myself away. My entire world was being turned upside down and inside out and more so with every passing minute. I thought that once the sales trip was over I would regain a little stability. I had hoped that once I was off the road and back in the familiar security of my own home that the severe anxiety, confusion and feelings of fear would slowly diminish and go away. But they weren't diminishing or going away, they were growing by the hour.

I stayed in my apartment for two or three days (I don't remember exactly for how long) fighting off wave after wave of anxiety, fear, and outright panic. I had no work until the following Wednesday when I had a sales meeting scheduled with my father, the president of the company, so I sat, I paced, and I tried to think. I had to think. But I couldn't hold a coherent thought. I couldn't piece together anything. Everything was falling apart, and I was like the helpless Dutch boy before the crumbling dike; one finger trying to block this hole and the other hand trying to block that hole while the entire dike is coming down and washing him away.

Words alone cannot express the shame and embarrassment that I felt the following Wednesday morning when I entered the office and had to confess to my father that, as far as I could tell, I was losing complete control of my mental faculties and had no reason why. Of course he was greatly concerned, anxious, and willing to do whatever he could to help me. He suggested an immediate visit to our family doctor, a man we both held in great esteem and confidence. After a hurried conference we left immediately for his office.

Waiting those few minutes to see the doctor in his reception room seemed like an eternity. I was so engulfed by the all-consuming symptoms that I was literally jumping out of my skin. All I could do was pace the office and with all my willpower fight the uncontrollable urge to run out the door and down the street.

After what seemed like an eternity the doctor ushered us into his office. He gave me a quick physical examination and questioned me about the symptoms I was experiencing. I told him about the lightheadedness, the dizziness and the strange feelings of disorientation. In all honesty there was no way to thoroughly describe what I was feeling and what was going on. But it was obvious that something was wrong, terribly wrong.

After our short consultation he deduced that somehow, something had happened to my internal state of balance. Somehow the internal sense of equilibrium between my mind and body had been drastically thrown off and it was due to this that I was feeling dizzy, lightheaded, and disorientated. Accompanying this disorientation was an incapacitating fear that manifested itself in panic attacks. Through the fog of my ongoing fear and confusion it almost made sense to me, oversimplified yes, but by that point I was ready to grasp on to anything that resembled a cure or a way out of the nightmare that I was living. The doctor prescribed Vistiral, a muscle relaxer, lots of rest, and another appointment in two days to check my progress. He went on to assure me that although

I was feeling terrible right then, that everything would be alright after a few days of rest. In fact, he said that I would be feeling as good as new in no time.

After the doctor's office my father took me directly to the pharmacy where I bought and immediately took a dose of the prescribed Vistiral. Afterwards we went to my parent's house where I had decided to stay for a few days until I felt better. I took the medication religiously every six hours and tried to rest and relax but it was of no use. The dizziness, lightheadedness, tension, fear, and confusion only continued to mount. I couldn't rest, I couldn't relax, and I couldn't do anything to abate the escalation of my strange symptoms.

I was unbounded again, like on the course, only this time it was not a feeling that made me happy or complete or connected to everything and everyone. It was the opposite: an uncomfortable, disconnection that went beyond feelings, mental definitions or anything that amounted to the concept of good in the world. I had totally lost that sense of "I" again, but now had absolutely no sense of any self or of this reality as we know it. I was looking on in mute terror as the walls of this reality softened, dissolved, and melted away as I slowly but surely moved into a vague, formless world without boundaries. And with this experience I could now sense other dimensions and other realities coming into play around me; spirits, strange energies, and phantoms just beyond my periphery gliding past me and whispering in my ears. That very thin hold I still had and was desperately trying to maintain on reality was slipping away. It actually felt as if this dimension was getting ready to collapse and I was going to be subject to that unknown and undesired peripheral world. It was going to consume me.

After two days of this horror I returned to the doctor's office, this time walking the two-mile distance alone through the rain. Sitting there in the waiting room, a new depth of depression and hopelessness washed over me. The doctor's theory about the cause of my condition was obviously incorrect and the medication that he had prescribed had not worked at all. Now I felt beyond the reach of modern medicine and certain that no one would be able to help me. I also felt certain that I was losing my mind. New, even darker waves of fear, panic, and depression engulfed me. Suddenly I jumped up out of my seat and bolted back out into the rain.

12

TODOS SANTOS,
GUATEMALA, 1999

*Releasing Kundalini without proper preparation
is like opening Pandora's Box without having
cultivated the ability to master what emerges.*
SWAMI RAMA

WHAM, BAM BAM BAM, WHAM BAM BAM! What the hell is going on? It sounds like someone is holding an automatic assault rifle to my ear and squeezing off rounds. Besides that, the bed is bouncing up and down and turning my stomach to the point of making me think that I might have to begin the day outside vomiting. I open my eyes and check my watch. Holy cow, it's seven a.m.! What time did I go to bed, two in the morning? How many beers did I drink, twelve, fourteen? Looking past my watch, my arm and further down the bed I see Cristina and Anita jumping up and down on the bed. They're screaming and giggling with delight. "Market, market, market, its market day! Get up Eric and take us to the market, we want to go shopping with you! There's fruit, avocados, sweets, pineapples, EVERYTHING! We want to go, come on, get up Eric, let's go!" The rapid-fire shooting noise is, of course, the *molina* situated right next door, grinding out corn for the neighbor's early morning tortillas.

Oh, I can't believe this, I am in serious pain. But miraculously, as hungover as I am, I do feel good; relaxed and centered in a foggy, sort of way. And besides that it is market day in Todos Santos, the weekly shopping, buying, selling and socializing frenzy that trumps all others. I shake Cristina and Anita off the bed with the promise that I will be along shortly then get up, quickly dress, and am out the door into a bright blue, high mountain morning. I take a minute to scan the surrounding mountains, take in a deep breath of fresh air, hit the bathroom, dunk my head in a basin of frigid water, shave, and head for the kitchen.

I don't see Anna or Ron around anywhere but there's Polo, already at the sewing machine churning out bags and pants for the tourists who are sure to arrive for the market. "Eric, you've finally awoken, you slept really late today, (they usually get up about five or so) is everything O.K.?" I give him a dirty look without comment and go into the kitchen to see what Nicolasa has cooking on the fire. "Eric, you've finally gotten up, we were worried, it's so late," she says. "Yes Nicolasa, it's very late I know, I'm just a little tired from all of yesterday's travel. What's for breakfast?" I ask, as I settle into a chair close to the fire. Nicolasa giving me a quick smile pulls the youngest Mendoza child off her breast, whips him around to his sleeping place in the shawl tied to her back and pours me a steaming mug of coffee. After coffee she serves me homemade tortillas with eggs, beans, and chilies to complete the morning meal. Finishing my breakfast I light up the first cigarette of the day, thank Nicolasa, promise to buy her some things down at the market and head out to take a seat in the sun next to Polo.

Sitting there in the morning sun next to Polo I can feel the eggs and tortillas starting to settle and the coffee and cigarette starting to wake me up and just in time because here come Anita and Cristina again. "Eric, Eric, Eric, let's go, it's already nine o'clock, they're going to sell everything before we get there!" "Okay, okay, I'm ready", I tell them and then I'm off to my room to get some money while they grab their shopping bags and the shopping list from their mother. Back in a flash, I grab them both by the hand, tell Polo that we will be back in an hour or so and then we're off skipping down the cobblestone street.

After a short walk down hill towards town we round a corner just above Main Street and run smack dab into the bustling market. The streets of Todos Santos are alive, jammed with Indigenous shoppers sporting the traditional pink, red and blue garb of Todos Santos and haggling over prices. Though quite a bit smaller than the San Cristobal market it is ten times more congested and has an almost exclusively Indigenous clientele. This is definitely a market for the people of Todos Santos (as opposed to tourists or *Ladinos*) and is full of locally grown corn, beans, fruit and vegetables, coffee, sheep, pigs, and everyday household necessities such as soap, pots, pans and so forth.

Anita and Cristina are jumping up and down with delight and can barely contain themselves. They want to see, touch, feel, and buy everything in sight. We squeeze our way through the violently pink and blue colored crowd discussing all of the things we see. Then slowly but surely we begin to shop, buying avocados here, (because they're cheaper) and tomatoes there, (because they're fresher). Next come bananas, flat bread, peanuts, onions, oranges, mangos, chilies, and finally a pineapple as we work our way down the list meeting neighbors and chatting. The final stop is the snow cone stand and a cool treat for all of us as the temperature begins to soar.

While resting in the shade and slurping our snow cones I spy Anna and Ron making their way up the street and hail them over. They too have been doing a bit of shopping, as attested to by their full bags, and eagerly accept our invitations to a snow cone. This is Anna and Ron's first trip to Todos Santos and they, like all tourists who make it up here (as I did three years ago), are thrilled and impressed by the beauty of the surrounding mountains and the experience of living so intimately with the Indigenous population.

"Holy cow Eric", shouts Ron above the surrounding din, "this is so incredible. I've never seen anything like it before. I love it here and can't wait to see what Nebaj is like. I want more of this, as much as I can get!" "Yeah", chimes in Anna. "This is fantastic and we definitely want to see some more of the same. We've been thinking about hanging out here a few more days before heading out to Nebaj on Thursday or so. How does that sit with you Eric?" "Sounds good to me," I tell them. We agree to gather around the map and a few beers tonight then they set off on a long hike. Back at the house Polo and Nicolasa are busy selling pants, bags, and shirts to the passing tourists so I drop off the girls, stow my purchases in the shed, grab my day pack, and take off up the mountain for a little exercise and a better view of town.

Right out in front of the house is the small lane that leads past the ruins (three small pyramids set in a tiny basin of emerald green grass) and up to the Indigenous village of San Juan Atitlan, five hours away. I went all the way to San Juan three years ago and it is a beautiful hike but my goal today is only the first ridge top one hour's hike above Todos Santos. I exit the Mendoza compound and start up the mountain, passing the ruins and the last huts and farms on the edge of town. Almost immediately I start to feel stiffness in my legs and back. After fifteen minutes of walking uphill I am breathing hard and have to stop for a few minutes to rest. It's been a while since I've hiked and I can feel the stagnant energy holding me down. After a few minutes of rest I'm back in gear and plodding a soft, steady pace up the mountain. Another ten minutes of steady climbing and I begin to find my hiking and climbing rhythm. I pass a few more isolated huts and a lady from Todos Santos leading her flock of sheep up to greener pastures. Now halfway up the ridge, I can still see Todos Santos and the valley far below. I stop to take another quick rest and for the first time see clouds moving up the valley and into position over Todos Santos.

While resting, I am passed by a small group of men on their way back to San Juan. These gentlemen and other market goers from San Juan, got up at 2:00 AM this morning and walked the five hard hours from San Juan to Todos Santos. After arriving in Todos Santos at 7:00 AM, or so, they spent the early morning hours buying, selling, and chatting away with friends. By 10:00 AM, business done, they hoisted their loads, often fifty pounds or more, and started the five-hour return trip to San Juan. They smile, wave, and pass me at the vigorous pace that comes from being born in these mountains and walking these trails since childhood. Taking a few moments more to let them pass and advance up the mountain, I shoulder my small backpack and start up the trail myself.

With the altitude gain comes a coolness accompanied by a faint breeze. I stop for a moment to put on a sweater before taking on the last three switchbacks to the ridge summit. Rounding the last switchback, I cut up to the left, and two minutes later am on the summit that marks the boundary between Todos Santos and San Juan. The view is spectacular! I can see all of Todos Santos and the entire valley below as if I were studying a map. To the left I can scan the valley back down to San Martin and Concepcion. Off to the right, I can see the single lane road that threads its way up the opposite ridge to the top of the valley that leads to Huehuetenango. Behind me I can see a deeply-forested valley and another ridge top with the trail to San Juan. Still farther away, I am able to locate various Guatemalan volcanoes and even two just over the border in Chiapas.

I take a seat, pull out my lunch of fruit and bread, and bask in the glory of it all. I am on top of the world, free and unfettered, without a care, the past a million miles away and the future but a faint rumor. Even when the clouds start to roll in and blot out the sun thirty minutes later they can do nothing to dampen my spirits. On the contrary, they are a welcome change to the bright sunshine that has been assaulting me all day.

Sitting with my back against a rock I watch as the clouds reach the ridge top and roll over the summit in a white wave to hide the valley below and surrounding ridges. Suddenly everything becomes quiet, deathly quiet it seems, the temperature drops another ten degrees, the cloud blanket thickens, and I find myself totally immersed in the impermeable thick, white silence that surrounds me.

It is absolute nothingness and in that nothingness I encounter all possibilities and a peace that lately I have only been able to find in my late night drinking sprees. And then I hear a voice speaking from above, calling, beseeching. I strain to hear it better but it recedes and then disappears altogether. Suddenly I hear another sound in its place; a bell, a simple bell. And with that bell comes a small parting in the clouds where I see Todos Santos again and closer, a flock of sheep coming up the ridge, the source of the bell. I stand for a moment and the clouds bow before me, part wider and disperse on their journey up to a distant ridge top.

With their departure the sun returns so I take one last glance around, reluctantly shoulder my pack, and begin to head down the mountain. Arriving back at the Mendoza's an hour later I feel revitalized from the climb but also ready for an afternoon nap. Avoiding the main house I sneak into the unoccupied shed and bury myself in my sleeping bag for a well-deserved rest.

13

PORTLAND, OREGON, 1989

*Into deep darkness fall those who fol-
low action. Into deeper darkness fall those
who follow knowledge. There are realms
of no joy, regions of utter darkness. To
those worlds go those who in their unwisdom have not awakened to the Light.*
THE SUPREME TEACHING

AFTER RUNNING OUT of the doctor's office and escaping into the rain that day I was at a complete loss as to where I should go or what I should do. I found myself wandering for hours in the pouring rain with the overwhelming symptoms as my sole companions. Finally, I ended up in a deserted church as a last resort where I sat piecing together what was going on. If I could only find out what was going on I could figure out a solution. There had to be some kind of explanation for what was happening to me.

Somehow, in the midst of that dark, swirling mental abyss I had the dim realization that the terrible nightmare I was living was directly related to the wonderfully positive experiences three months earlier in the ashram. In relating them it seemed there was only one thing to do: I had to get back to the ashram even though I had no idea what I would do when I got back there. In fact, the thought of going back, leaving and losing everything I had: job, career, relationships, and savings scared me to death, especially in my present state of mind. But what was the alternative? I needed to get out of the mental state I was in as soon as possible or something terrible was going to happen. I was absolutely certain of that. The thought of returning to the ashram, scary as it was, at least gave me a ray of hope, a direction and a chance to escape from the strange symptoms that were assaulting me. The mere thought of returning and all the planning involved helped to divert my attention from the horrors of the present.

Ten days later I found myself at the Portland airport waiting for a flight to the ashram on a rainy, gray afternoon. The last ten days had been nothing short of a miracle. In that short span of time I had managed to confront my father, explain the complexity of my problem as best as I could, resign my position in the family business, sell off or put into storage all of my possessions, and buy a one-way ticket back to the ashram. The devil is a mean taskmaster.

After an incredibly long and difficult flight from Portland I found out that the last bus for the ashram had departed an hour earlier and that my only option left, if I wanted to make it to the ashram by that evening, was to hitchhike. With night falling I walked down to the highway and stuck out my thumb in the beginnings of a full-blown blizzard. Luckily, after a short wait, a car pulled over and I traded the cold, wind and falling snow for a late model, luxury automobile. The driver was not going directly to the ashram but he could get me close, about an hour away. "Good enough," I remember thinking for by then I knew that the act of moving, progressing in the direction of the ashram was giving me focus and a welcome break from the symptoms that were assailing me.

Two hours later my ride dropped me off at a junction where, after another twenty-minute wait, I was picked up by a truckload full of college students who were going right past the ashram. I quickly climbed into the back of their pickup and once again was traveling through the falling snow and darkness, me with four others, huddled under blankets and bedding. An hour later we arrived at the gates of the ashram where they dropped me off and disappeared into the night.

I wish I could say that I felt relief upon arrival. And maybe I did feel a bit of relief, if only relief after a long journey and the knowledge that I had finally had made it to the ashram. There, at the gates of the ashram I halfheartedly gave silent thanks and trudged through the snow and darkness towards a friend's house in the tiny town adjoining the ashram.

Gentry Shumar was a friend of mine I met when we both arrived at the ashram as new students. He was now just finishing up his degree. I called him a couple of days before I left Portland and he agreed to let me stay in a trailer he had near his house. And that's exactly what I needed just then, time all alone, time to try and rest and relax, time to try and figure out just exactly what was going on and, most importantly, how to stop it. Hopefully, after a bit of rest and recovery I could petition to re-enter the ashram and really get to the bottom of what was going on and somehow return to the life that I had known before.

Arriving at Gentry's door he received me kindly enough but immediately remarked how tired, drawn, and haggard I looked. Oh how I desired to tell him the truth! My heart ached to tell him everything, to relate to him my tale of terror and all that had happened the last three months since the course ended. Looking back, maybe I should have told him everything, but at the time I truly felt that I couldn't. I was too confused, too far outside of this reality and living in that all-consuming distorted mental state where nothing made sense anymore. I could barely walk and verbally form sentences. How was I going to explain this to someone? And who was going to believe me? I could barely believe it myself. No, I thought, better to keep it a secret until I could find a way out on my own.

So I lied to him. I covered up the truth and told him I was tired from my heavy workload and the long trip back to the ashram. Yeah, I was beat, I said, and needed a week or two of rest and quiet before I re-entered the ashram. He looked at me for a moment and with a smile, handed me the keys to the trailer, told me he understood, and let me walk off into the night with the understanding that we would talk after I had rested for a few days.

Arriving at the trailer on the outskirts of town I remember thinking that now everything would be alright. I remember thinking that somehow, now that I was close to the ashram and had a place to be alone and relax for a while that I would figure out what was going on and return to a normal state of consciousness. For the first time in weeks I actually felt the smallest glimmer of hope and hint of relief. I stowed my gear, settled into the trailer, and tried to get some sleep.

The next few days I spent pacing the small trailer, trying to recognize myself in the mirror while attempting to remain rational, reasonable and of a sound mind, but it was difficult. Not only were the panic attacks and intense mental confusion continuing, they were increasing in intensity and there was nothing I could do to lessen their effects. My whole system of thought, comprehension, ability to perceive, control, reason and direct thoughts, was evaporating and being replaced by a swirling madness of nothingness. That small glimmer of hope that I had felt on arriving now vanished as if it were a puff of smoke on a windy day.

14

Todos Santos, Guatemala, 1999

I am Sacred, I am Glorious, I am Truth in all of its magnificent terror. Love me, worship me, praise me and adore me in the early morning sun and soft light of the moon. Send me offerings and oblations, promises and resolutions. I am creator, preserver, and destroyer of all, ever present yet seldom seen, often sought yet seldom found. I am your best friend and your worst enemy, your most precious dream and your most fearful nightmare, your crucial designer and your ultimate destroyer.
THE LAUGHING RIVER OF DRAGON FIRE

I WAKE FROM my *siesta* to the sound of the *molina*, wander into the yard, and run into Anna and Ron just returning from their hike. They're wasted from the six-hour effort up a ridge on the opposite side of the valley and ready for a nap and a *chu* (traditional Indigenous sauna) later on in the evening. We again make plans to go over the map tonight then they're off to have a rest while I wander over and take a seat next to Polo while works away at the sewing machine. One by one the Mendoza children return from their various chores and Nicolasa rekindles the evening's fire in the kitchen as darkness and night slowly consume the little valley. Alternating between the sewing machine and the *molina* Polo keeps himself busy while I make myself comfortable and begin to study the map for this latest adventure that we are about to begin.

Finally closing up the *molina*, Polo retakes his seat next to me, lets out a low whistle, chuckles and says "Boy, Eric, you sure got drunk last night." "Me? Holy cow, Polo, you were so drunk I practically had to carry you home!" "I wasn't really drunk Eric, I was only pretending to be drunk so that you would not feel so bad yourself about being so drunk." "What in the world are you talking about Polo?" "That's right, I wasn't drunk at all and to prove it to you I invite you to drink a beer with me right now. I invite you, you are my guest." To refuse would be an insult so I allow him to fish twenty *quetzales* out of one of the sewing machine drawers and send Jaime up to Dona Angelina's for the first round of evening beers. And so it begins again, another round of beers with my friend Polo Mendoza on the bench, at the sewing machine in Todos Santos, Guatemala. Around 7:00 PM, Anna and Ron emerge from their nap just as Nicolasa announces that dinner is ready, so we all cram into the kitchen and partake in a hearty dinner of chicken, beans and tortillas. After dinner Anne and Ron are off to take their sauna while I return to the bench, the map, and a few more slow beers with Polo at the sewing machine.

"Hey Polo, what do know about this road that supposedly goes from up here near the top of the pass all the way to Nebaj in the Ixil Triangle?" "Oh, that's a very dangerous place Eric, many, many bad people, many thieves and robbers, very, very dangerous, you shouldn't go there." "So you've been there Polo, you've traveled there before?" "No I've never been there, it is too dangerous for me to go, very, very dangerous, many, many thieves, and assassins too, very, very dangerous." "Then you know people who have gone there, you've talked to people who have gone there and told you what it's like." "No, I don't know anyone who has ever gone there but it is a very dangerous place. The people are very, very bad." "Well Polo if you've never been there and never talked to people who have visited there how do you know it's so bad and dangerous?" "Everybody knows that it is a bad place, Eric, and full of bad people. Better that you don't go there. Better for you to stay here where everyone is good and it is safe." "But Polo I don't understand, how can you say these things if you've never been there?" "I just know and now it is better not to talk about these things, someone might be listening."

Right, Polo, now I'm totally confused. Totally confused until I remember all of my previous experiences with the Indigenous people of Chiapas and Guatemala, which reminds me of the fact that if they are asked about something and they don't know the answer, they will almost always make up some kind of answer just to satisfy your curiosity and not appear too ignorant. That and a firm belief that everything apart from their immediate town and vicinity is extremely dangerous seem to be the common way of thinking around these war-torn mountains: ignorance and semi-justifiable paranoia.

I leave it alone for the moment but decide to spend the next few days questioning everyone I can in town about the route and what we can expect. A couple of minutes later Anna and Ron emerge from the Sauna and after dressing, come over to review the map. I don't want to mention what Polo has just said so I tell them I don't really know that much about the route, but it appears we should be able to wing it through in a day or two and find Nebaj somewhere on the other side. I am guessing there should be sufficient traffic to hitchhike part of the way and hike the rest, but if worse comes to worse we can always turn around and come back to Todos Santos. They are not worried in the least. In fact, they are up for the adventure and confident we will be able to find our way through. We agree to leave in five days, Thursday, and with that call it an early night.

Over the next four days I talk with everyone I can in town to try and get some idea as to how the route goes, what to expect, and how long it could take us. I get quite a lot of information, everyone seems to know the route, but unfortunately all the information is conflicting. Some say there is a road, others say there isn't. Some say there is traffic, others say there isn't. Some say it will only take five or six hours, others say three or four days. Some say that there isn't anyone up there, others confirm Polo's information that it is indeed a dangerous route. By the end of the four days I have no better idea what to expect.

Wednesday night during our last discussion of the trip before leaving I tell Anna and Ron all that I have heard and declare that I still want to go. They too admit to a strong pull of adventure and feel confident that if anything really difficult comes up we should be able to handle it. We also agree on another thing. Instead of waking up at four or five in the morning and starting the hike with a two or three hour uphill trudge to the cut off at Tres Caminos, we will sleep in and catch the 6:00 AM bus up to the cut off and start hiking from there.

The next morning we all get up early, have our coffee, say goodbye to Polo and the family, and catch the 6:00 AM bus towards Huehuetenango. It is a slow, steep ascent up the valley on a bus full of half-asleep Todos Santeros on their way to Huehuetenango. But after forty minutes we arrive at the crossroads of Tres Caminos and to the surprised looks of the bus driver and ticket seller, and in fact to all of those on the bus, ask to be let off, in the middle of nowhere. Actually it isn't the middle of nowhere because there are a few trucks parked at the crossroads, a small store too and, lo and behold, even a tiny restaurant. Quickly we scramble off the bus, enter the restaurant to more surprised looks and order more coffee and a breakfast that consists of *carne asada*, beans and, of course, tortillas. Talking with the waitress we find out that the village of San Nicolas and the trail to Nebaj is about a five-kilometer walk along the dirt road out behind the restaurant. As to whether or not we will be able to hitchhike or walk from San Nicolas onward to Nebaj, she has no idea. We will just have to wait and see when we get there. After breakfast we hoist our packs and start following the trail out behind the restaurant.

It is now about 7:30 AM and though it is still cold it is light enough for us to follow the trail that weaves along the top of the *altiplano* (high altitude, treeless plateau). Small houses and farms are scattered along the trail but now we are leaving Todos Santos behind and traveling through an area where the people, though still Indigenous, have chosen to leave their traditional dress behind and clothe themselves in modern, Western style clothing. Numerous side trails branch off from the main trail and each time we have to ask someone which is the trail to San Nicolas. Each time we get the same strange looks and inquiries as to why we are going that way. People can't fathom why we, Western tourists, would want to travel along this virtually unknown route. Luckily, after a half-hour or so, we meet a gentleman who tells us that he lives on the outskirts of San Nicolas. He says he will be more than happy to accompany us as far as his house and then there, point us the way to San Nicolas proper.

We trudge on mile after mile. The waitress told us it was only about five kilometers to San Nicolas but after almost an hour and a half of walking the village is still nowhere in sight. I ask our guide how much further it is to his house and the village and his reply is, "just a little bit further," followed by a smile and a wink. Finally, after almost two full hours of crossing the treeless tundra our guide tells us we have arrived at his house and that the village itself will be found, "just a little bit further down the road." We thank him and set off again traveling for another half-hour or so until, all of the sudden, we see in the distance what looks like a collection of huts big enough to be considered a village.

Our arrival into the village another fifteen minutes later is a shock to say the least, as it is totally deserted! There are enough small shacks and huts to house almost 500 people, but as far as people themselves, we can't find a soul. The whole place is empty and has a vacant, eerie ghost town feel to it; completely abandoned except for a few stray dogs and a chicken or two. We all look at each other, shrug our shoulders and continue walking along through the deserted, vacant streets.

Arriving on the other side of the village we all breathe a sigh of relief upon seeing a large truck in the distance, a road, and what looks like a store with actual people walking about. We hightail it over to the truck and road and ask the driver if he is going to Nebaj and can give us a ride. "No", he says, he is not going to Nebaj, he is going to Huehuetenango and with that he climbs into his truck, guns the engine, and takes off down the road in a cloud of exhaust fumes and dust. Well, if he went that way, vaguely west, then we must be heading in the other direction, vaguely east. Just to make sure I enter the store and ask if the road east leads to Nebaj and if we can expect any more traffic along the way.

What I find out is not encouraging. The fourteen-year-old boy behind the counter has no idea if the eastward road actually goes all the way to Nebaj. In fact, he has only heard the town mentioned a few times before, has never been there, and has no idea where it actually is. Worse still is the fact that the road to the east, which we are planning on taking, peters out after two kilometers or so and becomes a one-lane track suitable only for horses and foot travel. "Is there any other road around here that I might be missing? Maybe one that leads to Nebaj?" I ask. "No *Señor*, there is only the one road, no more," the boy answers. Disappointed, confused, and feeling more than a little lost, I rejoin Anna and Ron who are talking to some farmers they met along the road. The farmers assure us that the road will definitely eventually get us to Nebaj. But as far as hitchhiking, that is out of the question until we can get to a small village called Palope, some eight or ten hours down the road. Actually, one farmer says it's a ten-hour walk, another one says it's about a twelve-hour walk and the third thinks that it will definitely be more than a day's worth of long, hard foot travel. When I ask them how far it would be in miles or kilometers they all look pretty confused for a moment until one of them assures us that it is only about twenty or twenty-five leagues, which is a big help to us. What the hell is a league?

But at least we are heading in the right direction and know that Nebaj is out there somewhere. Whether or not we will be able to get there before nightfall is the next question. We are about 2,000 feet higher here than in Todos Santos and that means that it is going to be getting very dark and cold at about 5 or 6:00 PM. Ron is the only one with a sleeping bag so that means we have to get somewhere, at least to Palope, whatever that has to offer, by nightfall. It is about 10:00 AM now so that would give us about eight hours at the most to get to Palope, a supposedly ten to twelve hour to twenty-five league walk away. Besides all that I have very serious reservations about being in these mountains after dark. This is a wild zone, there are no police here, no army, no law, just *altiplano*, mountains, scattered, isolated villages, and God only knows what else. And last but not least, we only have a vague outline map of the Cuchamatanes with no trails marked.

Still undecided we huddle up to discuss our options. I want to carry on but at the same time there are too many tricky variables to make it a sure thing. Anna and Ron though want to forge ahead and give it our best shot. That surprises me but their enthusiasm is infectious, so after a short conference we agree to proceed with caution but at a good pace. If worse comes to worse and we get stuck out in the middle of nowhere at nightfall we will just make a big fire and hope that there are no bandits lurking about.

Luckily, there are houses along the road leading out of San Nicolas where we can ask directions to Palope. And indeed a few people know the way. They assure us that we are on the right track and need only follow this same road to get there. After a mile or so, the road turns into a dirt trail and the houses start to thin out and then vanish altogether. We are now all alone hiking up a small, open valley and moving in the direction of a small unknown village called Palope and civilization hopefully somewhere on the other side. Luckily, again, every twenty minutes or so, we come upon a *campesino* (farmer) traveling towards San Nicolas and each time I question them about the route to Palope. All of them say Palope lies somewhere up the road and that it is possible to arrive by this trail. This is encouraging.

After about an hour we come upon two little Indigenous girls tending their sheep. I question them about the route and direction too, but they just shrug their shoulders and laugh. Then they say something that I find very strange: "*Mucho cuidado por que la gente mas adelante son muy, muy malos y les van a quemar. Les van a quemar y les van a sacar los ojos con palos.*" Anna and Ron who are still not quite proficient in Spanish ask me what the girls have said. I tell them that the girls have told me that we are on the right track, which is a lie. I just don't have the heart to tell them that the two innocent, young girls tending their flock have just warned me, as Polo had back in Todos Santos, that the people who live ahead are very, very bad and are going to burn us to death and then poke out our eyes with sticks.

15

THE ASHRAM, 1990

*Unsafe are the boats of sacrifice to go to the
farthest shore; unsafe are the eighteen books
where the lower actions are explained. The
unwise who praise them as the highest end
go to old age and death again. Abiding in
the midst of ignorance, but thinking themselves wise and learned, fools aimlessly go
hither and thither, like blind led by the blind,
wandering in the paths of unwisdom.*
THE UPANISHADS

IT FELT LIKE I was standing chest deep in a rushing river. The current was that strong and rushing against
me at full force as I strained to keep from being
washed away downstream, over the falls into oblivion. It was a losing battle though, because no matter
how hard I tried to stay balanced, the torrent kept

coming, throwing itself against me without mercy. That was exactly what it felt like. Only the current that was assaulting me wasn't water, it was pure consciousness rushing at me, into me, and through me, washing everything away as I held on for dear life.

I was trying to write my name, on the application form to get back into the ashram, but it was turning out to be much more difficult than I had planned. In fact, it wasn't really working at all. I could remember my name, or at least I was pretty sure that I was remembering it right. But somehow the transmission of information from the memory center in my brain down my arm and to my writing hand was not taking place. The connection was completely lost between the two. If fact, my whole mind-body connection was disintegrating, falling apart!

I was in the personnel office beginning the application process to get back into the ashram. The first step was to fill out a form with my basic personal information and work history. After that I had to get personal recommendations from two people, long-term members who were on the ashram's governing council, then wait a week while all of the information was reviewed and processed. I knew I was going to have to go through an application process to get back into the ashram. I also assumed that even in my highly altered state of consciousness I could fake my way back in. But even the simple act of reapplying was turning out to be much more difficult than I had expected.

By that time my nervous system and my mental perceptions were cross-wired to such a degree that I could barely walk and talk, let alone do something as complicated as fill out a form. My brain was slowly dissolving into a blank of nothingness as I watched helplessly in mute horror. All of the memory banks of events, past history, and functioning abilities were being erased, dissolved by the energy that was still entering into my body at the base of my spine, rising up to my head, rushing into to my brain, and creating a dizziness, faintness, lightheadedness, and severe disorientation. I could not function in this world anymore. I wasn't in this world anymore!

Complicating matters was the amount of shame associated with all that was going on. I really needed to talk to someone. I needed to tell someone what was really going on: the depth of the problem I was facing. But to reveal the truth and depth of my problem to family or friends seemed, at that point, impossible. I simply didn't know how or where to begin. Even if I did know where to begin I did not want anyone to know what was happening inside of me.

In the end I had to take the next step. I had to move forward, into exploration, inquiry and investigation. As difficult as it was and as much as it scared me I simply had to do it. I made my way over to the campus personnel office and scratched my way through the entrance application, something that normally would have taken me ten minutes but in my present state took over an hour.

That same day I went in search of two friends and asked them to act as my sponsors. I had to get written recommendations from them, present those recommendations to the personnel office, and wait a week or two for all the information to be reviewed. I was able to find both friends that afternoon on campus and get them to promise to deliver their recommendations to the personnel office sometime later that day. They too commented on my state of nervous exhaustion, but once again I told them it was due to excessive work and related travel back in Portland.

Later that day, back at the trailer, as I began the waiting process to see if I would be accepted back into the ashram, a new set of fears assailed me. How long would it be until I was accepted? What if my application was rejected and I couldn't get back into the ashram? What if, what if, what if, became my newest demon as I waited and worried. Finally, after more than a week of unbearable anxiety, I got word that I had been accepted and could move into a room on campus the next day.

The ashram itself was situated on an old college campus originally built over one hundred years earlier and meant to house and educate almost 1,500 students. It was spread out over almost 262 acres of land, complete with ample brick housing, administrative offices, large kitchens, dining facilities, and separate buildings for group meditations that consisted, on the average, of up to 2,000 participants twice daily. Beautifully kept gardens, grounds and two small lakes with a fountain completed the scene.

The ashram, separate monastery and nunnery, and fully accredited co-ed university all occupied the same campus grounds creating a lively atmosphere with monks, nuns and students from all over the world. I was accepted back into the ashram's work-study program, living in separate quarters with the other monks on a secluded corner of campus, working for the university during the daytime and studying at night.

On my arrival back to the ashram I was assigned to work in the campus kitchen where I had worked years earlier and that suited me fine. First of all, because it was familiar; I had worked there two and a half years earlier and not only knew the routine but was also pretty sure I could at least follow through with the physical aspect of the job, even in my highly altered state. Second of all, with the intense work, noise and the large amount of new applicants into the ashram that would be working in the kitchen, it was an excellent place for me to blend in. I could just focus on my cooking, a job I knew well, have minimum contact with others, and hope that my condition would go unnoticed. Also the physical labor might provide an outlet for all the crazy energy that was racing through me. As exhausted as I was I also recognized the need for some kind of outlet at that point, some way to get rid of all of the bizarre energy that was coursing through me and eating me alive.

On the first morning I woke, bathed, did my morning meditation and sutra program alone (I had still not been cleared for group meditation) and got dressed for breakfast in the main dining hall. But all of the sudden I couldn't leave my room. Out of nowhere the ever-present symptoms escalated to new heights and I was engulfed in new waves of fear and panic. What had I been thinking of? There was no way I was going to be able to make my way through an entire day interacting with people at work. I was going to break down, be discovered and thrown out of the ashram. And then what would I do? Where would I go? How would I ever find out what was happening to me? That small amount of confidence and relief that I had felt the night before evaporated into a fine mist before my eyes, transforming itself into a host of phantoms that attacked me without mercy.

16

CUCHAMATANE MOUNTAINS, GUATEMALA, 1999

Long is the night to those who are awake;
long is the road to those who are weary.
Long is the cycle of birth and death to
those who do not know the Dharma.
THE DHAMMAPADA

AS WE CONTINUE hiking up the valley I try to forget what the two young girls have just told me back down the trail. I also try to forget what Polo told me back in Todos Santos. It is just too beautiful of a day to worry about murder and death or even their possibility. The sun is shining, the birds are singing, there isn't a cloud in the sky and we are hiking through some of the loveliest backcountry I have seen since my arrival in Central America almost five years ago. And besides, we have more immediate things to think about; namely getting up this valley and somehow finding our way through this maze of mountains to a village named Palope, hopefully somewhere on the other side. But so far so good, I'm just hoping that luck stays with us and we don't get lost.

We keep following the well-defined main trail that we picked up in San Nicolas, and as far as I can tell, it appears to be the main road-trail all the way to Palope. But then sometime around noon we reach the ridge at the top of the valley and find ourselves faced with the first real problem of the day: a perfect fork in the road with two trails heading in almost opposite directions. We now have a dilemma. Since this morning we have been either following a clear-cut route or been able to find someone to give us directions; but now, here at this fork in the trail, we are all alone out in the middle of nowhere with no idea which trail to take. One obviously leads to Palope, but where the other one leads and which one we should take, God only knows.

Feeling a bit perplexed by the magnitude of the decision, feeling a bit tired from the walk and heat of the glaring sun, we all decide to sit down and take a break. We find a bit of shade under a small tree alongside the trail and pull out water, fruit, bread, and cheese as we begin to discuss our options. Going back is out of the question. No, we are now committed to the other side and forward is our only choice of direction. But which trail to take? It is impossible to find any clue or hint as to which trail might lead us to Palope and where the other one might go. If only there was a house nearby or a *campesino* walking down the trail that we could get directions from. But the last houses we saw were almost an hour back down the valley, and as far as people, we haven't seen anyone since the two little girls tending their sheep back in the vicinity of the same houses.

We start debating which trail has the better chance of leading us to Palope when suddenly I hear faint footsteps coming up the trail behind us. A few seconds later a man comes around the bend. Startled at first he quickly regains his composure, smiles, waves hello, and comes over to join us.

His name is Pablo and he is a *campesino* returning to his village somewhere five hours or so up the left fork of the trail. He is returning from Huehuetenango where he has gone looking for work without luck. Being poor and without an income he has walked to and is now returning from Huehuetenango on foot, not having the six *quetzales* (eighty cents) to pay for the bus. I ask him about the two forks, where they lead and if he has any idea which one will lead us to Palope. "Have you ever heard of Palope?" I ask, and we hit the jackpot. Pablo has lived in these mountains all of his life. He has traveled the many trails extensively and has walked to Palope and even all the way to Nebaj numerous times. Not only can he give us directions to Palope, he can personally guide us to the town itself. For Palope lays a mere one-hour walk past where he will have to turn off to go to his own small village of San Augustina. Immensely happy and relieved at solving our dilemma, we invite Pablo to sit down with us and share our lunch.

During our meal, Pablo informs us that we still have a long way to go if we intend to get to Palope before nightfall. Quickly finishing our meal, we pack up our things, take the left fork of the trail, and begin the descent into another small valley. As we move down the valley at a brisk pace, me struggling to keep up with Pablo, Anna and Ron falling behind but within sight, I ask Pablo all about his village, about Palope, about the mountains he calls home, and about the people that live here. Pablo turns out to be a fountain of information and I listen attentively to all he has to say as we quickly work our way down through the short, tight valley. Rounding a bend we come into sight of another, larger valley below us, at least a half-mile long and maybe a quarter of a mile wide, treeless and threaded by numerous small streams.

Descending further down the trail we round another bend and get a still fuller view of the basin spreading out below. We can now see horse herds grazing below and off to our left as well as a few scattered houses climbing up the hills on the opposite side of the valley. Descending to the valley floor we come across a contingent of Indian women washing clothes in one of the many clear, sparkling streams. Pablo and I take a minute to talk with them as we allow our eyes to wander out onto the plains and the numerous small horse herds grazing and running about. A few minutes later Anna and Ron show up a bit winded but as surprised and happy as I am to find this hidden paradise in the middle of nowhere. We talk with them and the Indian ladies for a bit more and then Pablo and I set off across the valley with Anna and Ron once again following behind.

Fifteen minutes later we reach the other side of the valley and thread our way through two small hills and out onto another, larger plain that lies behind. From here, in the distance, we can see a small grouping of houses, enough of them and close enough together to possibly be considered an actual village, the first since San Nicolas now almost three hours back down the trail. I ask Pablo about the place. He confirms it is a village and that there is a small store there where we can purchase soda, snacks, and cigarettes. Instantly invigorated by the thought of a Coca-Cola and a cigarette I pick up the pace and twenty minutes later enter the small village.

Pablo says the village is called San Sebastian and that it is the largest settlement we will encounter until we reach Palope another five hours down the trail. The place looks to contain about forty scattered shacks, or so, but once again it appears to be rather deserted for the middle of the day. I ask Pablo about this and he explains that most of the people are out in the fields working and will not return until nightfall. We continue through the nearly deserted village until we come to the middle of town where, after dodging and wading through a gauntlet of barking dogs, we arrive at the store and set our packs down on the wooden front porch.

The owners of the store are an ancient Indigenous lady, her two daughters and a gaggle of children, grandchildren, ducks, piglets and puppies. They are as surprised to see us as I am to find them out in this wilderness. The small children, upon seeing me, shrink back into the folds of their mother's skirts and their mothers back into the safety of the store. Too thirsty to worry about manners or pleasantries I go inside, grab a room temperature Queen-Cola, pop it open, take a big swig and grab a cigarette from the package open on the counter. Lighting my cigarette I walk back out the door and scan the back trail searching for Anna and Ron. A bit concerned but not enough to worry about it, I return to the wooden porch and begin a conversation with the Indigenous lady and her two daughters who, with Pablo's reassurances that I will not bite or rob them, have emerged from the store along with the majority of their children and grandchildren and retaken their seats.

It is now almost 2:00 PM and we've been on the move since 6:00 AM; eight long, hard hours with about four or five more to go. I sit and talk for a bit with the reluctant family and Pablo until suddenly the dogs set off into a howling din announcing the arrival of Anna and Ron. Anna's still looking pretty fresh but Ron looks beat. I ask them how they're holding up as they come up to the store and they both acknowledge being a little tired, but still fit and ready to go. They put down their packs, nudge their way past the crowd and go into the store for something to eat and drink. We take another fifteen minutes resting at the store, pay our bill, and reluctantly head eastwards towards Palope. Although it's still early in the afternoon, clouds are beginning to roll in and the temperature is dropping. The bright, sunny day we have been traveling through is now turning into a cool, darkening afternoon that gives even more urgency to our arrival to Palope.

Leaving San Sebastian behind we continue moving through valley after winding valley, Pablo keeping up the steady, strong pace that he has been holding all day, me struggling to keep up, and Anna and Ron already falling behind. Every half hour or so we come upon another small group of huts that once again seem deserted but in reality are only empty for the day, the inhabitants off in the fields working. Pablo doesn't stop or even slow down as we pass these by, but merely shouts out the names of the various villages as we breeze past at our steady pace. We pass the next five miles or so winding our way over ridges, down through valleys and past the occasional deserted village. Finally, after about two hours of steady walking, we decide to rest for a bit, and wait for Anna and Ron who have by now fallen way behind.

During the height of the Guatemalan Civil War in the 1980's, the Guatemalan army constructed a garrison in the valley where we are now seated. The garrison was put here to restrict and block guerilla movements through these valleys that run between the department of Huehuetenango back behind us and the Ixil Triangle. Pablo points to the actual location, about fifty yards down the valley, where the garrison stood until just a few years ago. I am amazed to be sitting in this valley imagining the things that must have gone on here in years past; clandestine guerrilla mobilizations, roving government patrols, actual battles, and reprisals. It's hard to believe such violence could have happened in such a beautiful, peaceful place as this. But it did, for years and years without end.

In fact, it actually started more than 490 years ago with the arrival of the Spanish conquistadors in the early sixteenth century and their attempts to conquer and enslave the original Indigenous inhabitants of the Cuchamatanes, the Highland Maya. The conquistadors were swift and brutal in their methods and within a few short years the majority of the Indigenous population of the Cuchamatanes had fallen under their yoke and were either killed or enslaved. In the years and centuries that followed the Spaniards continued with a brutal system of domination that consisted of intimidation, slavery, theft, rape, torture, genocide and out-and-out murder as a means of controlling the Indigenous population. The Maya, faced with incalculable misery, hardship and possible extinction, fought back the only way they knew how: through secrecy, clandestine guerrilla warfare and revolution.

The beginning of the cruelest and most recent war started in the aftermath of a 1954 coup after which a succession of military presidents, working in conjunction with the church, major business interests, and the United States government, undid all of the political and social reforms that were then beginning to occur for the first time in the history of the country. Violence, oppression, and murder once again became the mainstay of Guatemalan political life as the rich, powerful and corrupt minority took full control of the country oppressing the poor, illiterate majority. As the pressures within Guatemalan society and politics increased so did the violence and resulting government repression which led to an even greater polarization between the corrupt rich and Indigenous poor. By the 1960's new, progressive guerilla groups began to form and a full-scale revolution began to take shape.

Slowly but surely building in power and intensity throughout the sixties and seventies, the war began to take a large toll on the poorer classes and Indigenous villagers. By 1980 it was estimated that approximately 60,000 people, mostly poor Indigenous civilians, had been murdered during the political violence of the previous decade. The early 1980's brought a peak of suppression and atrocities by the army and government against anti-government elements and Indigenous civilians. During that decade incredible numbers of people, again mostly Indigenous males, were kidnapped, tortured and murdered without a trial or even formal charges being brought against them. The Guatemalan Highlands, of which the Cuchamatanes constitute a large part, became a killing ground as the Guatemalan army, backed by a corrupt Guatemalan government, began a scorched earth policy of genocide and destruction in the hopes of erasing all possible Indigenous support of the guerillas.

The atrocities committed by the Guatemalan army during the early 1980's read like accounts of Cambodia's mass murders during the late 1970's: over 400 traditional Mayan villages burned to the ground, 15,000 civilian deaths and 200,000 refugees seeking exile over the border in Mexico. In the department (state) of El Quiche alone during 1982, fifty-four massacres were reported accounting for more than 3,000 civilian deaths. As one Guatemalan army Colonel, Carlos Arana (the butcher of Zacapa) Osorio, put it, "If I have to turn the entire country into a graveyard in order to pacify it I will not hesitate to do so."

The extended bloodbath finally led to a cutoff of all U.S. military aid to the Guatemalan government, which in turn led to the election of a civilian president, as opposed to a military dictator, for the first time in years. Slowly but surely things started to calm down with the approach of the 1990's and the decrease in military campaigns in the highlands. In the early 1990's a new civilian president, Jorge Serrano Elias, reopened a dialogue with guerilla forces in hopes of bringing the decades old war to an end. Then in December of 1996 a peace accord was finally reached between guerilla forces and the Guatemalan government formally bringing to an end the forty-two-year-old civil war.

In the end, the statistics of death and destruction among the Highland Maya were appalling; thousands upon thousands of innocent people tortured, raped and murdered. Thousands more merely "disap-peared" without a trace. More than 600 traditional villages and their ancient way of life were burned to the ground, erased or moved and altered to the point of being unrecognizable. The number of human rights violations are beyond counting. And yet still today, even after the signing of a peace accord, the Highland Maya of the Cuchamatanes are still struggling for the freedom and equality that was taken from them almost 500 years ago.

17

THE ASHRAM, 1990

We are shaken by secret shudders and dark fore-
bodings; but we know no way out, and very few
persons indeed draw the conclusion that this
time the issue is the long forgotten soul of man.
CARL JUNG

I GUESS IN the end it must have been the lack of options that got me to my feet and sent me down the
trail towards my first day of work. Far too anxious and
disturbed to go in the front door and eat breakfast in
the main dining hall, I went around to the back door
of the kitchen and immediately went to work. Thank
God I knew that kitchen well and what was expected
of me. I got my work assignment from the head chef
and launched myself into preparing one of the day's
vegetarian dishes. All I had to do was focus on the
recipe, follow the instructions, avoid contact with my

co-workers, and somehow I would make it through the day.

The kitchen was a hive of activity. Besides myself there were five other cooks, a head chef, a food services director, a caterer, a store man, six people in the bakery, four dishwashers, twenty people cutting vegetables and preparing food for the cooks, and a staff of servers and rovers to carry food to the main and satellite dining halls. It was a madhouse of noise and confusion, the perfect place to hide and the perfect vehicle for me, in my present state of mind, to get through my first day of work back in the ashram. But by day's end I was exhausted. All day long I had kept myself as busy as I could to deal with the symptoms. I hauled 100-pound sacks of rice, I stirred gigantic bubbling cauldrons of dahl with spoons the size of oars and I hauled steaming trays of food to the servers. I ran and sweated and looked for more work, afraid to remain inactive for even a moment.

After six hours of manic activity though, I was completely finished. I had spent the entire day burning off all of that strange energy that was racing through my nervous system like a wildfire, but in doing so had also burned up all of the energy that I needed to fight off the on-going symptoms and panic attacks. I was so wiped out when I finally quit working and sat down for a moment that I had serious doubts I would be able to walk the 200 yards back to my room without falling apart. Furthermore, I couldn't remember where my room was, which seemed ridiculous because I knew that campus like the back of my hand. Focusing my thoughts as best I could I was able to remember the general direction I was supposed to go, but drew a blank on the exact location of my room. I couldn't even remember being there in the morning or what it looked like.

Slowly getting to my feet and gathering what little strength I had, I started off in the direction of where I thought my room might be. Never before had I begun a journey that seemed so long or difficult. Slowly I put one foot in front the other until suddenly, shear panic grabbed me again. What if I couldn't make it? What if I couldn't find my room? What if I ended up aimlessly wandering the campus forgetting my name and everything else? These were very real possibilities for me that day. I had just the thinnest grip on reality and after the day's intense physical activity I was starting to lose it.

Arriving half-way back to where I thought my room might be and the dirt road I had to cross to get there, I was faced with the same dilemma from the morning; how was I going to get across the road? For even though there was almost no traffic on the road I was gripped with the mortal fear that I would be hit trying to cross the road by some unseen car or truck. Standing there on the edge of the road I looked first to the left to assure myself that no one was coming from that direction and then looked to the right. But then my distorted and irrational mind latched onto the unrealistic fear that maybe while I was looking to the right someone had come up on the left side and vice-versa. I stood there for a good minute or two looking back and forth, trying to get across the road hoping that no one was observing me. It was ridiculous and I knew it but it was the best I could do in my present state. Finally, in desperation, I threw caution to the wind and walked across the road hoping no one would hit me.

"This is so ridiculous", I remember thinking, as I continued searching for my room. I had been there only hours before, I knew that campus and I knew where my room was. But it wasn't just a simple matter of remembering and then finding my room. Those memory banks and my ability to access them were not functioning anymore. Those parts of my brain were now either severely impaired, completely erased, or in the process of becoming so. And in fact, as the days went by, I found myself unable to access more and more things, memories, and basic functioning information. It was all slipping away.

Finally, through trial and error I eventually found my building and my room. But opening the door and entering my room was like entering it for the first time. I recognized nothing! Those were my things in the room, or at least they were supposed to be, but it was like I was seeing them for the first time, totally unrecognizable. So how could I be sure that this was my room? My name was on the door but shouldn't I recognize something? And how could I really be sure that that was my name? I thought so, but I wasn't sure. I went over to the mirror and looked at myself in it, again, totally unrecognizable. I knew it was supposed to be me but in all honesty I had never seen that person in the mirror before in my life, a total stranger. So who was I looking at then? And who was I, a total stranger looking at a total stranger in a totally new and strange land? Too confused and exhausted to even begin piecing it all together, I fell into bed without even contemplating supper. I only wanted sleep and oblivion.

18

CUCHAMATANE MOUNTAINS, GUATEMALA, 1999

All actions take place in time by the interweaving of the forces of Nature, but the man lost in selfish delusion thinks that he himself is the actor. But the man who knows the relation between the forces of Nature and actions, sees how some of these forces of Nature work upon other forces of Nature, and becomes not a slave.
BHAGAVAD GITA

FIFTEEN MINUTES LATER Anna and Ron come into view from back down the trail. They're moving slowly and Ron seems to be limping. When they finally make it up to where we are resting it is all too apparent that

Ron is in pain. I ask them how they are doing and Anna replies that she is still feeling really good but Ron admits to fatigue and blisters on his feet. I ask Pablo how far we still have to go and he says that Palope is still a fair distance away, two hours by his reckoning, which really means about three hours. I ask Ron if he thinks he can walk three more hours. He grimaces but says he can. Part of the problem is his pack. Anna and I are carrying minimal gear, having left the majority of our things back in Todos Santos, but Ron is carrying his full pack, almost fifty pounds. I'm still feeling pretty good and know that the remaining trail will be mostly either flat or downhill, so I offer to trade my light fifteen-pound rucksack for his fifty-pound backpack. That agreed on, we rest a few minutes more and set off at an even sharper clip.

We cross the valley, traverse a few more, and top a large ridge before entering another large valley. We pass a few more deserted settlements with Pablo calling out their names (Las Piedras, La Ventana) as we rush pass. Finally we come to another fork in the trail where Pablo stops and informs me this is where he will have to leave us. Our trail to Palope lies straight ahead he says but the trail to his village turns off to the left. While we wait for Anna and Ron to catch up he tells me how to get to Palope: straight ahead to the top of this ridge before us then follow the top of the ridge to the left until we reach the head of the second valley. Once we reach that second valley we head straight down it until we reach Palope. He says that the trip should only take us an hour or so and that once we start getting close to Palope there should be enough people on the trail to give us directions. He's in a hurry to get home himself, still having four miles to walk, so I thank him profusely and wave goodbye as he jogs down the trail and out of sight.

After saying goodbye to Pablo I take a seat and wait impatiently another ten minutes or so until Anna and Ron come into view down the trail. They're still walking along at the same slow pace and I am getting annoyed because I know we have to move faster if we're going to reach Palope before nightfall. They arrive a few minutes later, Ron looking greatly pained, and I gently try to tell them the importance of picking up the pace. They agree to do their best and we set off up the ridge.

I take the point and move ahead, eager to see the lay of the valley on the other side of the ridge and someone who might guide us into Palope. It's a tricky business though, because without Pablo's steady guidance it's hard to determine which is the actual trail and which are merely spur trails leading off into the middle of nowhere. I find myself rushing ahead for five minutes and coming to a junction where I am forced to wait for Anna and Ron so we don't become separated.

I finally reach the top of the ridge, follow it eastward and come to what I believe is the top of the second valley that Pablo had mentioned. I search in vain for a trail leading down into the small valley but can't find one. When Anna and Ron catch up we all make a concentrated effort to find some sort of way down into the valley below, but we can't find anything. We have a quick conference and decide to continue along the ridge top trail until we can either find some kind of trail that loops back down into this valley or one that will lead us down into the next. But there are so many mountains, so many connecting ridges and valleys, maybe Pablo got his directions wrong, maybe I heard him wrong, or maybe I'm just mixing up valleys. Whatever the case, we have got to get moving because it's cooling off fast and complete darkness will be upon us in less than an hour. We move off quickly along the ridge top trail, me taking the lead once again, eager to find a trail that will lead us down into the valleys below.

Five minutes later I see two young girls ahead on the trail. I shout a hearty "*buenas tardes*" and almost run towards them relieved at last to find someone who can help us with information and directions. But as soon as they see me they run off into the bushes and scramble up the mountainside like two scared mountain goats. I forget that these mountains still carry the memories of almost forty years of civil war and that in these hills the word "stranger" still translates into enemy and danger.

Undeterred, I keep moving down the trail until I run into a group of men cutting firewood. Greatly relieved I move towards them slowly and cautiously this time. When I finally get close enough I say hello and ask them about the trail to Palope. They say, "Palope?" They have never heard of the place and have no idea where it might be. They are from a small village back over the ridge and have never even heard of Nebaj or the Ixil Triangle. I continue questioning them for a few more minutes until I realize they have no information that can help us then head back down the trail to make sure Anna and Ron are still coming up behind me. I backtrack for five minutes and begin to get worried. They can't be this far back. What with talking to the woodcutters, backtracking, and their forward movement I should have run into them by now. I backtrack another couple of minutes but still can't find them. I whistle and call out their names but only hear the hollow echo of my voice in response. I backtrack another fifty yards or so but find nothing except an empty trail, a jumble of other trails branching off into the murky forest, and descending darkness.

I stand there for a couple of minutes feeling frustrated and angry before realizing that won't help anything and take a seat on a log. I feel so helpless, so out of control. I have no idea where Anna and Ron are. I have no idea where the village of Palope is. I don't even know where I am! I mean, I know that I'm somewhere in the Cuchamatane Mountains of Guatemala but as far as an exact location, or a way back to civilization, I haven't a clue. It's actually a bit scary sitting there alone in the middle of nowhere with darkness descending. But at the same time I find it relaxes me a bit for the first time all day. I've been going so hard, so fast all day that the acknowledgement of being lost gives me the first opportunity of the day to really stop and look around. It's actually quite a beautiful evening; I'm in the woods at twilight with a perfect view down the valley that falls away at my feet, the birds are singing their last choruses of the day and the details of the trip become secondary to just being a part of the evening that surrounds me.

Suddenly I hear footsteps coming down the trail and turn to see Anna. "Eric, there you are, we've been waiting for you back down the trail. Where have you been?" A bit shocked at the abrupt end to my silent reverie but relieved to see her, I tell her about getting lost and running into the woodcutters who knew nothing about Palope. She hurriedly explains to me that they have run into a *campesino* who told them Palope is in the valley behind us. In fact, all we have to do is backtrack back to where she left Ron and take a spur trail down into that valley. She left Ron only five minutes back down the trail so we double time it back to him and start looking for the trail. But there doesn't seem to be a trail, and worse yet, we see no signs of a town in the valley below. Despite this we decide to bushwhack our way down through the brush in hopes of finding a trail. The going is steep and difficult, but after a few minutes the trees start to open up offering a better view down into the valley. We still can't see Palope but we can see some farmhouses, smoke rising from their chimneys, and a man working in his field. Encouraged and excited by these newfound signs of civilization, we tumble down the steep hill onto the farmer's field.

If Martians had dropped out of the sky from a space ship it would not have surprised this poor Indigenous farmer as much as our sudden, raucous appearance in his potato field at twilight. Upon seeing us he automatically grabs his hoe, goes into a defensive position and starts to back up towards the safety of his house. Quickly I shout out hello and start to slowly move towards him while explaining our predicament and asking for directions to Palope. Seeing that we have a woman with us he stops retreating, puts down his hoe, and relaxes. When we finally reach him he is still shaking a bit but has calmed down enough to converse with us. Yes, Palope, he knows it well. It lays a mere fifteen minutes or so down the trail that starts below his field. Relieved to be so close to our goal, we chat with him for a couple of minutes, thank him for his help, shake hands, and head off towards Palope.

The trail at the bottom of the field is well-defined and easy to distinguish from the feeder trails that branch off to the left and to the right. After a short walk it broadens substantially and we enter into a flat clearing with a few small adobe houses. We don't see anyone here but we can hear voices coming from one of the houses so we approach that house and shout out hello. Nothing for a few moments, so we shout again and a diminutive lady quickly peeks her head out the door and then back in again. Seconds later a man emerges cautiously and we ask him about Palope. "Yes, Palope, you are very close, a mere ten minutes or so down this trail and you will arrive. You are almost there." We thank him and set off again at a brisk pace.

Continuing down the trail it finally starts to level out a bit and the valley opens up. Scattered houses are now a common sight and the few women that we see peeking out from behind the doors and windows of their adobe houses wear the bright red *corte* and green *huipile* common to the Ixil Indians that inhabit this part of the Ixil Triangle. Startled at first by the drastic change in local dress, shock quickly turns to excitement as we realize that this change signifies our official entry into the Ixil Triangle, another world, and the outskirts of the village of Palope. Topping one last rise, we see the edge of town another hundred yards below. I am so excited I practically run to the edge of town to assure myself it is really there, that we have actually arrived. I cross a small bridge over a crystal clear stream and wait a few moments in the deepening darkness for Anna and Ron. Minutes later they join me and we walk into Palope a tired, dirty, ragtag trio of foreigners.

Upon entering the small village the dogs begin to howl and bark and we are immediately surrounded by children, a bit scared at first, but then leaping and dancing with joy at the novelty of strangers. Pablo told us there were no hotels in Palope, but that we might be able to sleep in the school and borrow some blankets. We head for the center of the village where we guess the school might be, answering numerous questions along the way from the growing mob of excited children that surround us.

Arriving in what appears to be the center of the village, we find a small store, drop our packs, and buy sodas to celebrate our arrival. We are all beat but Anna, feeling the freshest, heads up a small hill to where the children tell us the school lays while Ron and I sit on our backpacks and chat with the growing crowd around us. Anna returns a few minutes later with great news; not only has she found the school, but she met a gentleman who lives right next door to it who will rent us a room, let us borrow some blankets, and even have his wife fix us dinner. Happy and relieved to hear the news but too tired to get up, Ron and I continue lounging on our backpacks and sipping our sodas. Finally, at Anna's urgings we drag ourselves up the hill to the house of one Don Jose.

Don Jose is an Ixil Indian as are all the inhabitants of this small village of almost 300 people. He greets us heartily and, after showing us the small shack where we will be sleeping, invites us into the main house, a small one room building that serves as kitchen, living room, and bedroom. By now it is completely dark outside and the fire and a fifty-watt light bulb are the only light inside his adobe home. Smoke fills our eyes as we enter the room and take the pint-sized wooden kitchen chairs that Don Jose offers us. Looking around inside it is easy to see that the building is well over a hundred years old and made of all natural materials; adobe walls and coarsely hewn beams all lashed together with hand woven agave rope. Again it feels like we are stepping back in time a century or two.

Over the fire is Don Jose's wife, Esmerelda, who takes a few moments from her tortilla making to shyly greet us in the few words of Spanish she knows. Next,

Don Jose calls for his three pre-teen daughters. The very images of their mother in their bright red *cortes* and handmade *huipiles,* they bow one at a time and say their names in a mixture of fear, excitement, and curiosity.

While Esmeralda and the girls prepare dinner Don Jose pumps us for information about our journey, the United States, and Holland. At the same time we ask him question after question about Palope, the mountains we have just traveled through, and the trail to Nebaj. He says the trail we have just taken is not a common route but that foreigners who do take it sometimes turn up on his doorstep looking for a place to sleep. As far as the trail to Nebaj is concerned, we still have a way to go, one, maybe two days by his reckoning. Easier, he says, would be to walk down to Saquil Grande, a three hour hike, and from there catch the bus to Nebaj, an hour's ride over bumpy dirt roads. And besides he says, tomorrow is market day in Saquil Grande, so there will be a lot to see and do. We talk it over for a few moments and decide to do as he advises.

Dinner arrives in the form of tortillas, beans, canned sardines, eggs and coffee. Almost too tired to eat we manage to consume the majority of the feast while we talk with Don Jose and try to converse with his wife and daughters. Stuffed and exhausted we beg Don Jose to please pull out the blankets and lead us off to bed. It takes him a few minutes to go around to his neighbors and scrounge up spare blankets for us, but he finally returns with three thin blankets and leads us outside, through the cool, clear, star-studded night to the shed below his house.

Our beds are bare boards set on sawhorses but we are too tired to care. We are all just so glad to have survived the day, happy to be in this small, humble Indigenous village barely noted on the map and far, far away from the "civilized" world. Crawling into "bed" we talk for a few moments about the wonder and beauty of the day and the incredible changes that we have seen on the trail from Todos Santos to Palope. What a day! It feels like a month's worth of living in a single day. I keep talking until I hear Ron's soft snoring and turn to ask Anna a question but she is already fast asleep herself. Content beyond words, I pull my blanket around me to help fight off the chill, give thanks for the wonderful day, and then quickly fall into a deep, well-deserved sleep.

19

The Ashram, 1990

Awake! Arise! Strive for the highest and be in the light. Sages say the path is narrow and difficult to tread. Narrow as the edge of a razor.
Katha Upanishad

For the following days, weeks, and months that's how it went: ongoing disorientation, confusion, fear, out-and-out, non-stop panic attacks, severe exhaustion, and work in the kitchen. After my first week of work I received the official O.K. to join group meditations in the meditation hall. More than an O.K., it was an ashram rule to be in group meditation practice twice a day. Failure to fulfill this obligation meant inquiries, questions, and possible expulsion from the ashram. But I was looking forward to the group meditation sessions. I fondly remembered all of my previous experiences and had high hopes that the meditation and sutra program with the large group would have a positive effect of my condition. Once again I couldn't have been more wrong.

Why did I continue you might ask? Well, in the intensely agitated and confused state of mind that I was in, I truly believed that the meditation with the yoga sutras, the herbs and the marma aroma therapy were the only things keeping me from going over the edge. I was afraid to stop. A meditator now for over six years and practitioner of the yoga sutras for almost three, I had always taken great joy in and received great benefits from my meditation programs and Ayurvedic health care practices. I felt that stopping, would have only made things worse and that was a chance I simply could not afford to take.

Now my meditation-sutra program with the large group was deeper than ever before. Well, maybe not deeper than on the big course but surely different. The experience was like going deep down inside a bottomless, unknown, unending dark pit. I actually felt that I might go so far as to lose my way, become lost in consciousness, and not be able to find my way back into my own mind and body again. Just where I might go I had no idea but I was pretty sure that I would not be in my own mind or body or even in this realm anymore. And then, I thought, at the end of the group meditation, after the bell had rung and every-one else had gotten up to leave I would still physically be sitting there in my meditation pose but that's all that would be left, an empty, physical shell without a mind to go with it. That thought terrified me but what else was I to do? "Maybe this is the way out," I remember thinking. Maybe somewhere deep down inside of me I was going to find the answers that I so desperately needed. I was so confused about what I should do, how I could get better, that I was willing to try almost anything. And now that I was back in the ashram I thought that if I just followed the work-meditation program and kept my condition a secret something would turn up sooner or later and everything would work out.

Looking back, maybe I should have asked for help. I definitely could have used some! Somehow, due to all that had happened on the course, I had broken through the sphere of my own individual consciousness and into some kind of vast, unbounded consciousness that was far greater than anything I could have ever imagined possible and obviously way beyond my abilities to manage or even understand. For years afterwards I wondered why I hadn't reached out and asked for the helping hand I so desperately needed. Was it fear, was it shame, or was it merely as Kundalini expert Gopi Krishna says, that if and when the lone aspirant does accidentally break through into this almost unknown realm of human experience he or she must eventually resolve the problem on his or her own combined solely with the infinitely powerful grace of God? To tell the truth, I wasn't really sure. I only knew, had a sneaking suspicion or intuitive feeling you might say, that I was the only person I could completely trust with the strange situation I was in. So I didn't tell anyone else what was really going on but instead decided to blaze on alone through the strange, new, almost unknown world that I had accidentally entered in the hopes that somehow, somewhere the needed answers would come.

It actually took about six months, the spring of 1990, before everything slowly started to begin to make sense again. First of all I quit using the marma and aroma therapy oils that I had been using since the course of the year before. The six-month treatment plan was more than over and when I ran out of the oils I quit using them. Suddenly I started to feel better for the first time since the course ended. Still in a very precarious mind-set, I remember being surprised, greatly relieved, but also confused by this result. Encouraged by the slight improvement in my mental state, I also quit using the herbal preparation that I had been taking. Again, I felt a little bit better and was surprised by the results. No miraculous transformations were taking place but the acute anxiety and overwhelming mental confusion was starting to abate and that was the first good news in over six months.

The discovery that the herbs and the marma aroma therapy were actually causing my strange condition, or at least partially causing it, was a shock to say the least. But how could this be? In my highly altered state of consciousness I had been under the impression that these things were actually keeping me from going over the edge. But the results were right there before me; without the herbs and marma-aroma therapy I felt better than I had felt in six months and, more importantly, I was able to think clearly, make concrete observations, and begin to put some precious space between myself and the nightmare of the previous six months.

And just in time too, because by that point I was thoroughly exhausted. The physical cost alone took a devastating toll on my body; I had lost ten percent of my body weight and had a gaunt, haggard, look. I also had dark, heavy circles under my eyes and looked like some kind of ungodly wraith from the darkest regions of some nefarious other world nightmare. Every single day of the last six excruciating months was evident and all too obvious not only in my physical appearance but also in every aspect of my daily manner of living. In short, I was a vague shadow of the man that I had been six months earlier.

But now I finally had a little bit of solid ground under my feet. I finally had a very small, but vital grip on mental solidity again. I could sometimes think rationally again. I could sometimes remember things again. My brain and brain-body connection were beginning to work again. I could feel old emotions and reconnect with the various parts of myself from before the course and the madness that followed. I had begun to worry that I would never make it back to a normal state of consciousness again. But now I was finally beginning to see a light at the end of the long dark tunnel I had been traveling through the last six months.

20

THE IXIL TRIANGLE, GUATEMALA, 1999

Healing and demonstration take place as our minds become attuned to the truth of Being.
ERNEST HOLMES

THE THREE OF us wake up early the next morning still stiff from yesterday's long hike and a night of sleeping on hard boards. We're still a little bit tired too, but more than anything there is a shared sense of excitement and adventure about this journey we have only just begun. Yesterday's hike was fantastic, but finding this small valley and all but forgotten Mayan village is like something out of a dream. Now today we will go down the mountain and deeper into the Ixil Triangle, Nebaj, and the territories beyond. It is almost too much to contemplate and enjoy at once.

Anna, the first out of bed, grabs her towel and toothbrush and bounds up the hill to the village's communal washbasin for a good scrub. Ron, still a little groggy, decides to stay in bed for a while longer. I slowly pull myself up out of bed, have a good stretch, and walk outside. Once again the sky is clear and the sun is bright. Looking around I can see that the village of Palope is situated in a broad basin just below the head of the valley that we came down last night. Off to the left are steep hills and forest climbing almost straight up the mountainside but off to the right there is a good view of the mountains on the far side of the broadening valley. Even though I feel tired and stiff from yesterday's hike I cannot help but feel renewed by the beauty of it all. Suddenly Don Juan hails me from above and invites me up to the house for a cup of coffee.

Arriving at his house I enter the darkened adobe dwelling and am assaulted by thick wood smoke billowing up from Esmeralda's cooking fire. She's already busy patting out tortillas by hand, placing them on the grill, and turning and fussing over them as if they were her own spoiled children. A pot of beans and another of fresh coffee bubble merrily away to one side, but without breaking her rhythm she pours me a cup of the piping hot coffee and says good morning in her halting Spanish.

Sipping my coffee I chat with Don Juan for a bit, then go outside again to bask in the sun and breathe the early morning air. Up the hill, I see Anna at the community washbasin. She is surrounded by a crowd of village children who sit entranced by her every movement as she soaps and rinses out her hair. Down below, Ron has finally decided to get out of bed and I can see him shaking out and rolling up his sleeping bag. Don Juan pokes his head out the door to inform me that breakfast is ready, so I shout out to the others that it's time to eat and go back inside to see what's for breakfast.

A few minutes later Anna and Ron come inside and we all take seats around the fire and dig into a hearty breakfast of eggs, beans, tortillas, and coffee. During breakfast I ask Don Juan about the trail down to Saquil Grande and he assures me that it is an easy, well-marked, three-hour downhill walk to the small town where we can catch the noon bus to Nebaj. Quickly finishing our breakfast and coffee we pack up our belongings, hoist our packs, and head back up the hill to say goodbye to Don Juan and his family. Once again it is a difficult parting. The only way I can convince myself to leave is to promise Don Juan (and myself) that I will return soon. That done, we shoulder our packs and head for the other side of town where we pick up the trail to Saquil Grande.

The trail is, as Don Juan said, well-marked and almost all downhill, so we make good time and within an hour come out of the forested hills and begin to see individual houses, fields of corn and even a few small villages. The miles and minutes pass quickly and we all begin to warm up from the exercise, rising sun, and friendly company of the passing Indians we meet on their way to the market in Saquil Grande. After another hour or so, we come up to an old school house and take a short break for water and something to eat, in the midst of which, the Indigenous schoolteacher and her entire class of thirty twelve-year-old Indigenous students come out to chat with us and marvel at the rarity of our passing. We talk with them for a while, promise to visit the schoolteacher at her home in Nebaj, and hoisting our packs, wave good-bye and set off down the trail towards Saquil Grande.

A half-hour later we come upon the outer fringes of Saquil Grande. Houses are now more frequent and luxurious in size and style. Our trail has turned into an actual dirt road with a bit of traffic on it and there is an even steadier flow of *campesinos* accompanying us towards the market and town center. Fifteen minutes later we reach the town proper and begin winding our way through cobblestone streets, over small hills, and through narrow alleys following the lead of the numerous Indians in front of us. Finally, we top one last rise and see the town center and market below us. Entering the market we wade through the crowd, grab a seat at one of the food stands lining the market, and order something cold to drink.

We are all tired and overheated from the hike but the festive atmosphere of this new market has us off our stools and exploring all there is to see. A few minutes later someone informs us that the last bus for Nebaj is getting ready to take off, so we quickly search the market for the bus, squeeze on board (barely), and take our places in the packed aisle, all of the seats already being occupied. The trip to Nebaj is rather hot and uncomfortable standing up in the overcrowded bus, but the occasional glimpses of the surrounding mountains and countryside I am able to see out one of the dust coated windows more than compensate for the discomfort. Slowly but surely we travel along the bumpy dirt road swaying back and forth in the aisle until an hour later when we finally approach the outskirts of Nebaj.

Actually this is not my first visit to Nebaj. I had a one-night stay here just over three years ago when I arrived by bus from Todos Santos, via Huehuetenango, with a couple from Australia. We had planned to stay a week and then journey to the nearby villages of Cotzal and Chajul, but heavy military activity in the area between rebel forces and the Guatemalan army frightened my traveling partners so we left town the next day. I vividly remember that short but exciting stay in Nebaj; groups of soldiers on every street corner were carrying automatic rifles, grenades and machine guns; army helicopters arrived and took off with troops and supplies; patrols scoured the surrounding hills just out of town searching for guerillas and the town square itself was converted into the army's command post of operations. I found myself more excited than scared and wanted to stick around to see how the whole thing turned out, but my traveling partners insisted on heading out for someplace safe. The next morning we caught the bus and headed back down the mountain to the major tourist market in Chichicastenango and safer ground. I have always felt cheated by that first stay in Nebaj so I'm really looking forward to returning.

21

THE ASHRAM, 1990

He who conforms to the course of the Tao,
following the natural process of heaven and
earth, finds it easy to manage the entire world.
HUAI NAN TZU

AFTER ALL THAT I had been through, it felt like nothing less than a miracle to have the capacity to think clearly, remember, rationally perceive things and make good, sound decisions again. At last, the waves of fear and intense mental confusion were receding and I began to take a little joy and comfort in the simple things of life, things that I had always taken for granted. Things like eating, sleeping, having a normal conversation with someone, or just walking to work in the morning. I was delighted by how beautiful the simple pleasures of life really were. And I promised myself that I would never take them for granted again.

The life that I had known before, I could vaguely remember it again, not all of it, but bits and pieces for sure. I could feel it again, and also remember all of the great experiences of the course. I still had a long way to go as far as making sense of everything but I finally had a little space to think and perceive all that had happened from an observational point of view. I had a central point of reference at last! Something else that I had always taken for granted and never appreciated before or understood to its fullest degree.

Achieving that little bit of stability and clarity was a relief beyond words and finally opened the door to my recovery. Through trial and error I began to see that rest, low stress and consistency in my activity helped a lot to fight off the symptoms of my condition. And so that became my focus: consistency, low stress, and as much rest as I could fit into my schedule. In fact, the spring and summer of 1990 was a survival schedule that consisted of going to bed as early as I could, my two group meditations, a five-hour work day in the kitchen, and three quick meals, sometimes eaten alone in silence. What little time was left over I usually spent alone in my room trying to figure out what had happened and how I could accelerate the recovery process. Life was still extremely difficult, but I was recovering at last. I finally had a path, a concrete direction that I could trust and take out of the madness that had begun after the course.

With the partial return of my normal thinking processes and the ability to make clear, logical observations again, I began to question some of the ashram's teachings. Something was obviously wrong. There was definitely a problem with what I had been taught and my experience on the course. This was confusing, of course, because I previously had had such great experiences in the ashram. For years I had nothing but positive experiences. I had never thought to question anything or anyone. But now it was all too apparent that something was amiss, that some very important details were missing from the spiritual path they were teaching. But the vital questions were what exactly happened to me, what was still going on, and most important, what could I do to restore my mental state?

What I needed now more than anything else was just more of the mental solidity I was starting to achieve but I needed time now too; time to put as much space and solid ground between my new reemerging self and what had been going on the last six months. I needed to put it behind me so I could begin to reestablish confidence and trust with life again. But the memories were still all too vividly there. And in fact, just remembering the terrible onslaught of symptoms was enough to hurl me back into a state of panic so I had to be careful. I had to train myself, day by day, sometimes hour by hour, to watch my mind and be positive at all costs.

In October of 1990 I decided to transfer out of the food services division of the ashram and move to a less chaotic position in the campus press. It was time to start refining my still precarious recovery and I felt that moving from all the noise and activity of the kitchen into a quieter, more settled environment might have a positive effect on my still shattered nervous system. Two weeks later I began working in the campus press-room churning out tests and study material on a small printing press for classes on campus. It was definitely more laid back, there was a level of peace and quiet which is what I really needed at that time. I needed peace now, I needed quiet, I needed space, and I needed as little drama and personal interaction as I could get for a while. I needed to gear down my nervous system and brain from all of the powerful energy that had been coursing through me.

Fall blended into winter, winter into spring. My state was still tenuous but I was beginning to enjoy days, even weeks of clarity and stability woven in-between. I still took every opportunity I could to rest and further simplify my life in order to speed up my recovery. I also still shunned most social activities and group study as best as I could without raising suspicions. Instead I began to explore the campus grounds and surrounding countryside in quiet contemplation. In fact, it was at this time that I found myself inexplicably drawn towards nature.

Every free moment I had now I tried to spend out of doors walking slowly in nature and soaking up the deep silence, the simplicity, and something else I was finding there that was impossible to define. At the beginning of summer I found a few small lakes just off the campus grounds so as summer began to bloom in earnest I bought a fishing pole and in the evenings walked over to one of the lakes and sat on the bank basking in the stillness of the multi-colored sunset and the hope that a fish might rise. Recovery was slow, very slow, painfully slow actually, but I could definitely sense a recovery happening and that new mental stability continuing to grow.

I could finally breathe again. I could finally relax a bit and begin to believe that now maybe everything was going to be alright. And the better I felt the more I was drawn into the natural world and the magic I was finding there. It felt as if I had finally found something that I could relate to on a big scale if that makes any sense. For I had lost all of my connections, or at least abilities to connect with anything over the last two years, and I desperately needed to re-establish some kind of connection, some kind of relationship in the material world that was completely safe and serene enough for me to trust. In short, I needed to regain and reestablish trust in my life and nature provided that vital connection.

Still, to a large degree, I was in the dark regarding what happened to me and why. I was just barely beginning to learn, or relearn if you will, the fundamental skills of living and functioning in the material world again, almost like a new born baby learning to walk and talk. Yes, as strange as it must sound, I needed to reprogram and reboot my entire brain and nervous system. The incredibly bizarre six months after the course had either erased or severely distorted all of that information in my brain. So as far as the "what" "how" and "why" of the causes concerned, I was going to have to figure those out later as I continued to recover my complete mental faculties.

22

THE IXIL TRIANGLE, GUATEMALA, 1999

When all the knots of the heart are bro-
ken, then the mortal becomes immortal.
KATHA UPANISHAD 6.15

NEBAJ IS THE largest town in the Ixil Triangle and sits just above 6,000 feet on the northeast corner of the Cuchamatane massif with a population of about 10,000 mainly Indigenous inhabitants. Larger and more populous than Todos Santos, Nebaj also sports a few large hotels, a bank, and numerous restaurants. Before the arrival of the Spanish, it was the hub of the Ixil Indian's mountain empire and produced large quantities of high quality jade. Then came the Spanish conquest, often brutal in these parts, but it was not until the third attempt, in 1530, that the Spanish were finally able to take over the original town, burn it to the ground, and enslave it's surviving occupants. In the years that followed, the local Ixil population was regarded solely as a source of cheap labor by their Spanish conquerors, forced to work either as slaves or for bare sustenance wages on local coffee *fincas* (large agricultural estates) or distant coastal plantations which further decimated their population.

More recently the town of Nebaj, her sister villages of Cotzal and Chajul, and the other surrounding villages of the Triangle were hit by wave after wave of violence as the area became the main theatre of operations for the Guerrilla and the Guatemalan armies. Being the center of commerce and government for the entire Triangle, Nebaj played an important part in the war. In 1978 guerrilla forces regularly occupied surrounding villages where they held open meetings. In 1979 they briefly took control of Nebaj, holding meetings in the town square and killing Enrique Brol, a local landowner and abuser of Indigenous rights.

These actions brought swift repercussions from the Guatemalan government. They came into the Triangle and began to kidnap, torture, and kill villagers and suspected guerrillas. Things escalated as guerrilla forces launched a major counterattack against government forces, which were now firmly entrenched in Nebaj and the surrounding area. Shortly afterward, Guatemalan army chief of staff, Benedicto Lucas Garcia (the president's brother), flew into the area and summoned a meeting with the local Indigenous population. In a short, simple speech he warned the local Indigenous to either clean up their act or pay the consequences, the consequences being annihilation of the entire population. A few months later President Lucas Garcia was overthrown by a military coup and a new president, General Jose Efrain Rios Montt, came to power.

Rios Montt continued and in fact escalated the violence against the Indigenous inhabitants of the Cuchamatanes, making the sixteen months of his presidency the bloodiest in Guatemalan history since the original invasion of the country by the Spanish conquistadors more than 400 years earlier. In the short sixteen-month period of his administration tens of thousands of non-combatant farmers and peasants were killed by government death squads (at the height of the violence this number was reportedly 3,000 people per month) and over 100,000 rural villagers were forced to flee their homes. Hoping to erase all possible support for the revolution, Rios Montt instigated sweeping changes in the government's war against the guerrillas by establishing a new policy of using civilian patrols in place of army troops to protect local communities from guerrilla influence. At the same time the Guatemalan army began aggressive sweeps through the mountainous regions around Nebaj, Cotzal and Chajul, burning villages and terrorizing the local population before bringing them back to Nebaj to be resettled in "model villages" where the army could keep an eye on them. Slowly but surely the Indigenous community began to reject contact with the guerrillas.

As a result, the guerrillas' efforts in the area suffered greatly and they responded with desperate acts aimed at intimidating the local population and trying to win their favor anew. But with the army's new offer of amnesty to all guerrillas willing to surrender, combined with the continuous crackdowns on the guerrillas still hiding out in the mountains, the revolution's days were now numbered. By 1985, the majority of the guerrillas were either dead, had surrendered or were hiding out deep in the jungle or mountains. By the early 1990's the guerrilla movement was on its last legs and the war all but over. And now, just a few years earlier, the last of the guerrilla leaders have finally surrendered and what was left of their ragtag forces have come out of hiding and signed a final peace accord with the Guatemalan Government.

Pulling into downtown Nebaj and winding our way through the neat cobblestone streets and brightly whitewashed buildings it's hard to imagine such a recent, violent and bloody history here. Everything looks so peaceful and happy. And besides that, the three of us are too excited about our arrival to be thinking about past horrors and bloodshed. We have just spent two hard days hiking through some of the most remote mountains in the country and are ready to celebrate our return to civilization, Nebaj, and the heart of the Ixil Triangle. Arriving in the town square we bound off the bus and grab our packs as they are passed down from above. Taking a quick look around we all decide that what we really need is a round of cold beer. Shouldering our packs we head over to the

Restaurante Maya and order three cold, dark Moza beers before settling into a meal of fried chicken, beefsteak, rice, beans, and tortillas.

An hour later we order our third round of beer and start to make a game plan for our stay here in the Triangle. First of all we need to find a hotel and if I remember right the Hotel Ixil is a mere three blocks or so from the Restaurante Maya. I mention this possibility to Anne and Ron and they agree to staying there on my recommendation. As far as how long we plan to stay in Nebaj before moving on, we decide that three days should be enough. A bit of rest and relaxation today, tomorrow a hike over the hill to the village of Acul and then the next day, Sunday, we can visit the market here in Nebaj. On Monday we'll head off to explore Chajul and Cotzal. That decided, we pay our bill and head down the road to the Hotel Ixil.

The Hotel Ixil is where I stayed with the Australian couple three years ago and, upon returning, I see it hasn't changed a bit. An old colonial house like the Posada Casa Real in San Cristobal, it looks to be about 200 years old. Single-storied as opposed to the double tiers of the Posada Casa Real, it is also twice as large as the Posada Casa Real, complete with two plant filled patios. After taking a quick look around we rent a room for the three of us, stow our gear, and take turns taking nice hot showers and lounging around in the sun on the patio.

I take my shower, change into some clean clothes and stroll back into the office for a beer as Anna and Ron catch a few winks back in the room. A few hours and a couple of beers later they wake up so we take a walk through town looking at the sights, eventually ending up at the house of the school teacher we met on the trail from Palope to Saquil Grande.

Her name is Patricia and she is a full-blooded Ixil Indian wearing a blood red *corte* and handmade *huip-ile*. Patricia is twenty-five years old and after studying for three years at a university in Guatemala, accepted a post in the school where we met her earlier today. She greets us warmly and invites us in her house, which is almost a carbon copy of those in Palope and Todos Santos. At first Patricia seems a little embar-rassed and at a loss for words but a few minutes later her older sister Maria arrives from her house next door and invites us over to see some handmade hats, bags, belts, and vests she is hoping to sell us.

Entering Maria's house she takes us back into the bedroom where, from under the bed and out of the small wooden closet, she pulls gunnysack after gun-nysack full of handmade items. I myself am not too interested in buying due to almost five years of travel and purchase in Mexico and Guatemala. But Ron and Anna, being recent arrivals, are quite taken with the beauty of the proffered merchandise and so not only buy a good majority of the items that she has for sale, but order an additional quantity of hats and bags to take back home. Maria promises to have them done, with the help of some friends, before we leave in three days. Afterwards, we sit and chat for a while and then take our leave, promising to return in a few days to pay for the ordered items.

By now a cool, dark evening is starting to settle in so we head back towards downtown, find what appears to be a nice restaurant, grab a table, and order beers as we read the menu. The food here in the Triangle, and in Guatemala in general, is a far cry from what can be found north of the border in Mexico, but the chicken with rice that we are served more than satisfies our appetites. After dinner we order another round of beers and head back to the hotel where Anna and Ron go to bed early while I make one last trip to the store for a six-pack of Gallo beer and some cigarettes.

Back at the hotel I bundle myself up against the cold, grab my Walkman, and take a seat out on the patio in the darkness beneath the stars where I crack open a Gallo and light up a cigarette. Amidst the music, the beers, the cigarettes, and the stars above, my mind is racing along at a mile a minute. I am happy, incredibly happy for what we have accomplished over these last two days. I am also happy to be back in the Ixil Triangle so far away from the tourist hordes and deeply immersed in this ancient Mayan culture. The future also looks bright for we will be traveling into new and unknown territories all this week. Tomorrow we will take a three-hour hike to the village of Acul, a place I have never visited. After that, market day here in Nebaj, and the day after that we're off to Chajul and Cotzal, two villages I have wanted to visit for many years.

Chajul and Cotzal! They seem like distant, unattainable mirages even though we are so close and will be there in a few days. To go there, it is said, is to go back three, four, five hundred years in time. Proudly traditional, closed to outsiders, brave, free, strong and silent, Chajul and Cotzal were two of the hardest hit areas of the recent Guatemalan Civil War and to this day still remain two of the strongest guardians of ancient Mayan tradition. This is going to be an incredible week I think, as I pop open the third Gallo from my six-pack and light another cigarette letting Tangerine Dream and the Walkman rest for a bit so I can enjoy the silence and stars.

But I'm a bit worried, too. I've been traveling, moving, constantly running and drinking for four, almost five years now and it's starting to take its toll. True, it's been a lot of fun and a great help in forgetting what happened back in the ashram but I'm starting to get really tired and more than a little worn out from all of the late nights and constant travel. I want to go home now but I don't know where that is anymore. It's not back in Portland, Oregon and it's definitely not the ashram. Todos Santos, San Cristóbal, somewhere along the Pacific coast seated in a hammock? I have no idea.

Reaching for another beer I find that I have already finished an entire six-pack in less than two hours. That makes over two six-packs today. Far from an abnormal occurrence it is now an almost daily fact, as common to me as breathing, eating, or sleeping. I struggle up from my chair and look at my watch to see that it is a quarter past eleven. The office is closed, as well as all the stores in town but, experience has shown me that where there is a will there is a way. Grabbing my wallet I head out the front door confident that somehow, somewhere, I *will* find more alcohol even at this late hour, in this ancient Mayan village, deep in the Cuchamatane Mountains of Guatemala.

23

THE ASHRAM, 1991

That is, at bottom, the only courage that is demanded of us; to have courage for the most strange, the most singular and the most inexplicable that we may encounter. That mankind in this sense has been cowardly, has done life endless harm; the experiences that are called visions, the so called "spirit world", death, all those things that are so closely akin to us, have by daily parrying been so crowded out of life that the senses with which we could have grasped them are atrophied. To say nothing of God.
RAINER MARIA RILKE

IN THE FALL of 1991 I began to adopt a new style of living. I was beginning to realize I couldn't go back to the life that I had known before. No, too much had happened, too many big changes had occurred and too much water had passed under the bridge. I had simply seen and experienced far too much on far too grand of a scale to think I could go back to that simple, innocent, or rather ignorant life and mental framework that I had known before the events of the course. I was in a new world now and now that the intense transition of initial awakening had begun to recede it was time to decide what I should do next.

With the recession of the symptoms, the return of clarity, and the major shift that was beginning to occur within me, it was now starting to feel like I was being guided by an inner voice or inner compass. It was a feeling, a very distinct inner feeling, that now told me exactly what to do and when I was making the right decision and taking the right path and when I was heading off in the wrong direction. I was in touch with "Myself" again but it was a lot bigger and deeper "Self" than I'd known before the course. It was a lot clearer too and never hesitated to tell me what was going on and what I should do to get better. A lot of times it didn't make sense, at least in regards to my old, "before the course" way of thinking, but it always worked out for the best in ways I would have never been able to figure out on my own. I also had mental, emotional, and physical boundaries again, which was a relief after floating around in that intense, unbounded, indefinable energy of absolute non-existence. But these new boundaries also felt as if they weren't made by me but rather by some other force, a benevolent force, that was guiding me out of what had happened and into something new yet, safe, solid and nurturing.

As the days and weeks went by, a deep relaxation and new energy unfolded within me, something that started on the course but had very quickly gone beyond my ability to manage. But I had some perspective now. It finally felt safe enough to quit struggling against what happened, flow with it, and see just where it might lead me. Surrender, sweet surrender, maybe that was the answer now. And maybe, just maybe, I really had passed through the worst of it. My job now was to keep aligning myself with my recovery program of rest, nature, and this new energy, or rather intuitive feeling, that was guiding me out of the intense turmoil of the last two years and into a new world.

That fall of 1991 I quit going to the group meditation program and even quit doing the advanced sutra program I learned six years earlier. Instead I just did the simple twenty-minute meditation I learned in 1983 alone in my room. If anyone asked me why I wasn't in group program anymore I just told them I was sitting in a different part of the meditation hall now. It was a big place and there were lots of people; it was easy not to be missed. Again, I felt a lot more grounded and stable. Initially it was a tough decision to make because I had always enjoyed doing the sutra program, but right now I needed to back off for a while. "Back off," I say because I could now see I had gone way too far with the whole thing on the course. But now clarity and stability were finally returning, and with them the ability to see what happened on that course and what happened afterwards.

I had gone too far, way too far into something that was beyond my powers to comprehend or manage in any way. The extended meditations with the yoga sutras on the course, the marma aroma therapy, and the herbs had all come together to somehow open a very large door in my psyche and allow me to get a glimpse of a world that most people never even realize exists. Amazing stuff! Incredible stuff! And I, so fortunate to have seen it all! But it had simply been too much too fast. And even though I had been doing all of it under the supervision of my teachers, a lot of this stuff, and especially doing it in combinations like I had on the course, were relatively new to the Western world so I was pretty sure that even they weren't exactly sure what could happen. In fact, there was talk going around that they were actually trying out some of these new therapies on us to see how we would react, what kind of experiences we would have! Obviously my reaction was not what they hoped it would be. And I think it was my therapist afterwards who put it best when she said "it was like I was a ten amp fuse that received a 10,000 amp charge of energy and couldn't handle it. It was simply too much too fast and so I had blown a fuse, so to speak". Now I needed to cut back on what I had been doing in the ashram and try to stabilize myself as best I could.

Each morning now I awoke early, but instead of going to group program, found myself on a small hill staring transfixed as nighttime and the stars receded, dawn began, and the sun slowly rose over the far horizon and started the day. I would sit there in awe, amazed as I watched the entire process unfold. It was like I was watching the whole world begin anew. Evenings I would again be drawn outside where I gazed at the moon and stars rediscovering the sacredness, the grandeur I first discovered on the course. For me it was a new beginning and spoke of Eternity, the vastness of the universe, and the underlying ruling intelligence that runs it all.

Yes, I was coming back, I was definitely coming back now, the symptoms of disorientation and fear were entirely gone, but the reality that I was coming back to was like nothing I had known before. It was very similar to that which I experienced on the course but not nearly as intense. It was like a middle ground between that experience and reality as we know it. But I still had to be careful. If I did too much, became to immersed in superfluous activity, I would start to feel a little strange again, almost like I was taking a step backward into the symptoms. So I made sure that even when I started to feel completely recovered I strictly adhered to the basic principles of my recovery program.

24

THE IXIL TRIANGLE, GUATEMALA, 1999

Change and growth take place when a person has risked himself to become involved with experimenting with their own life.
HERBERT OTTO

I AWAKE THE next morning very hungover but in relatively fine spirits. Ron and Anna are still asleep so I have a quick breakfast of bread and fruit, wash it down with a Queen Cola and a cigarette and head out. I follow the streets down to the edge of town in search of the trail to Acul. Passing some pre-Columbian burial grounds I find the trail and start following it as it turns into a series of switchbacks and climbs out of town. The trail is steep and the going is tough but I revel in the hard exercise and sweat knowing that with each step I am leaving my hangover behind. Although still early, the sun is bright and I find myself stopping frequently to gulp from my water bottle and look back at the panorama of Nebaj slowly spreading out below me. After an hour of climbing I reach the summit of the small mountain and take a short breather.

A few minutes later I am off again and take about five minutes to work my way across the broad summit of the mountain to the other side. Reaching the other side I can see a small fertile valley below and what I believe to be the village of Acul. I start working my way down the backside of the mountain towards the village but it is a steep, difficult descent. Eventually the trail begins to level out and I enter the outskirts of Acul. Walking slowly into the village I can see that it is a much smaller and simpler affair than Nebaj, with a population of about 600. As I walk the main thoroughfare I don't see any hotels or restaurants, I don't even see any businesses or people walking about, just small, tile roofed adobe houses one after another in neat little rows. Reaching the village center, I see a few people milling about in the street and then, a bit further on, a couple of small stores.

I eventually come to the village square and a monument recently constructed by the Guatemalan government to commemorate the people killed here during the civil war. I study the monument and take out my guide book to read about the grisly evening of April 20, 1982, when government forces searching for guerilla operatives randomly chose and then herded twenty-four villagers into this square before killing and decapitating them as a warning to the town. Returning the next day, Guatemalan soldiers killed twenty-two more villagers and tortured others while numerous houses and farms were burned. I stand there for a few minutes in the bright, early morning sun. I try to comprehend all the violence so recently visited upon this village but can't correlate it with the beauty I see today. Realizing the futility of trying to understand it all, I say a silent prayer, and continue through town until I find the road back to Nebaj.

On the road back to Nebaj I keep an eye out for the cheese factory that the guidebook says is somewhere along this beautiful country road. Suddenly it's as if I have been transported to Switzerland, but not even these slow rolling hills, the bright green, flower-framed pastures or the abundant Swiss cows on this bright sunny day can help me forget all of the recent violence here in Acul and Guatemala. A few minutes later I see a small cluster of buildings off to the left and, taking it for what I believe to be Finca San Antonio and the cheese factory, I leave the main road behind and slowly work my way up the dirt road to the main house. I climb the stairs to the porch and knock on the wooden screen door, which is soon answered by a middle-aged lady. I tell her that I am interested in purchasing some cheese and without a word, she leads me over to a small barn where she opens a door and we enter a world of darkness and strong odors.

She flips on the light and I see two cheese presses and numerous shelves stacked with different shapes and sizes of cheeses, all marked and dated. She asks me what kind of cheese I would like to buy and I ask her what types she has and how much they cost. She rattles off a list of names and prices, none of which I am really familiar with. Sensing my ignorance and apprehension, she deftly pulls a knife out of her pocket and slices thin wedges of cheese off the various blocks for me to try. I try two or three and am surprised by their smoothness and mellow flavor. I eventually choose a quarter kilo wedge of the smoothest, pay her in *quetzales*, thank her, and walk back to the main road.

The guidebook says it's about twenty kilometers, thirteen miles, back to Nebaj along this road and, not wanting to retrace my steps back over the mountain, I follow the road in hope of catching a bus along the way, or hitchhiking back to Nebaj. I end up walking along the road and the banks of a small beautiful stream for another hour or so until I come to an intersection and a few Indians waiting for the bus that supposedly will be along in a few minutes. An hour later a dilapidated dump truck pulls to a stop and we all pile into the back, holding on for dear life as we are vigorously bounced along for a half hour or so and then left off on the outskirts of Nebaj. It takes me another twenty minutes or so to reach the hotel on foot. Anna and Ron are out so I have a snack of bread and cheese and take a nap.

A couple of hours later Ron and Anna burst into the room raving about their wonderful hike, the one I have also just finished, then sit down on the bed and begin to feed on their recently purchased cheese with bread, tomatoes, cucumbers, chilies and sips of Moza beer. I get up, splash some water on my face, accept a cheese, cucumber and tomato sandwich and then a Moza beer. After a couple beers each, and an ample sampling of our recently bought cheese, we go out for an early dinner then return to the room where we all read before turning the lights out early and going to bed.

The next morning we all wake up early and head back down to the Restaurante Maya for breakfast and then to the market. Today, market day, not only the market building and surrounding streets but actually all of this side of Nebaj, turns into a seething torrent of buying, selling, trading, and haggling over prices. Slowly but surely we work our way through the crowd marveling at the wide variety of hand woven clothes, bags, hats, fruits, vegetables and various items for sale. Three hours later we end our visit to the market with lunch in one of the many stalls.

After lunch we head back to the hotel where we make plans for a visit to Maria's house and tomorrow's departure for Chajul, Chajul being the first of the two villages we have chosen to visit as we move deeper into the Triangle. Afterwards, Anna takes off for a short walk, Ron decides to head back to the market, and I buy a six-pack of Gallo beer as evening begins, slowly sipping my beers and thinking about our departure for Chajul.

This is the real thing, real exploring, really getting out there. Few tourists come to Nebaj, but even fewer visit Chajul or Cotzal. I can't believe our good fortune and the week that lies ahead. Yes, sitting back and

opening my fourth beer I can already feel the excitement of our impending departure into the unknown.
Anna and Ron both return at about the same time so
I finish my last beer, grab my coat, and we all head
back over to Maria's house.

Maria is waiting for us out in front of her house and she
greets us warmly then invites us back to the house's one
bedroom where she pulls sacks out from under the bed
that contain Ron and Anna's order. A few minutes later
her sister Patricia wanders in and I chat with her while
Anna and Ron negotiate prices with Maria. Business
completed, we sit and talk with them for a while, promise to return after our trip to Chajul and Cotzal to pick
up the merchandise, and then wander back downtown,
have some dinner and head back to the hotel. Arriving
back at the hotel, Anna and Ron head directly to bed
while I go buy a few more Gallo beers and reclaim my
favorite chair out on the patio where I turn my Walkman
on to some Grateful Dead. Four hours and about eight
beers later I join them in a good night's sleep.

The next day we are all up early and ready for our
departure to Chajul. We shower, pack up our things and
have breakfast once again at the Restaurante Maya. By
8:30 AM we are finished with breakfast and standing in
front of the plaza waiting for the bus that supposedly
departs for Chajul at 9:00. It's another bright, sunny day
so we don't really mind the wait, but by 9:30 the bus has
still not arrived and we are starting to worry. I wander

around a bit asking people about the Chajul bus and, as always, get a wide variety of answers. Everything from "it already left earlier at 5 AM" to "it doesn't run anymore you'll have to walk" to "it won't arrive here until tonight but I don't know if it will return to Chajul." Feeling a bit frustrated, we decide to throw caution to the wind and start walking to Chajul.

Walking out of town back to the main road we take a right and follow the road towards Chajul twenty miles away. It's already starting to get warm so we walk for only fifteen minutes or so before we drop our packs beside the road and decide to hitchhike. Traffic is sparse, but twenty minutes later the Chajul bus comes huffing and puffing its way up the road. We flag it down and squeeze onto the overcrowded bus.

We are the only non-Indigenous people on the bus and I almost feel embarrassed in my health and prosperity compared to the poor, broken down Indians with whom we are traveling, the poorest I have seen yet in my travels. The three of us tower over the ragged crowd of diminutive Indians around us who, undernourished since birth and still surviving on a daily diet that rarely exceeds a small bowl or two of beans and a handful of tortillas, seldom exceed four and a half feet in height. We must look like giants to them, so tall and healthy in our bright, shiny clothes. We are free also. Free, happy, incredibly rich, by their standards, and unencumbered by years of war, poverty, intense fear, torture, and murder. Looking around at the sad, dirty faces that follow our every move and listen to our every word with ears that cannot understand is

mind-boggling. And they are all so quiet, so frightened looking. Only the very small children can manage a smile. These people, this countryside has so
many tales to tell, yet so many secrets to hide. Will we
be able to discover it all in the four or five short days
we plan to stay here? And if we do see it all, will we
be able to understand and accept it? These thoughts
and many more are running through my head as we
bounce along the slow dirt road on a bright sunny day
towards the distant village of Chajul.

An hour later we pull into Chajul and find it to be
not much more than a dirty collection of adobe huts
perched precariously on the side of a hill. Crossing a
small stream we see an ancient whitewashed church
towering over the surrounding huts and the village
square. Arriving at the village square in front of the
church, the bus pulls up to a stop and we tumble off
with the rest of the passengers. Immediately we are
surrounded by a group of pre-teen Indigenous girls
dressed in bright red *cortes* and blue hand-made
huipiles, (as opposed to the green *huipiles* of Nebaj)
all with ancient Spanish coins dangling from their ear
lobes. They are all chattering away a mile a minute in
a mixture of broken Spanish and Ixil; something about
wanting to take us to their various houses and show us
antique jade, coins, and other relics that their fathers,
brothers or uncles have found while digging in the
fields. It sounds interesting to us, so we agree to look
for them after finding a hotel.

We wander around a bit, with the same group of
small girls following behind us, until we find Chajul's

only dilapidated hotel. Paying two dollars each for a small, damp, dirty room, we drop off our bags and go back out into the street where the girls are waiting. "Come to my house, come to my house, come to my house first," they are all screaming in unison. Their enthusiasm and excitement are infectious and we can't help but be curious as to where they want to take us. We choose the tallest of the girls and go to her house first, promising to visit the other houses afterwards.

Her name is Rosa and she appears to be about twelve years old. She takes me by the hand and, with Anna and Ron following behind, leads us down the street and through a back alley where we arrive at one of the small adobe, red tile roofed houses that dominate the town. She yells something in Ixil through an open window and we hear an answer from the other side in the same guttural dialect and then what sounds like a flurry of giggles, whispers and movement from inside. A few moments later a woman opens the door, greets us in broken Spanish, and invites us inside.

It takes a few seconds for our eyes to adjust to the dark, smoke filled room, but then we can see that besides our guide and the woman we take to be her mother, there is also a group of six other children ranging in age from six to sixteen and two women with babies at their breasts who all watch us suspiciously from a dark corner. Rosa's mother whispers a hushed command to one of the older children and small wooden chairs are brought out for us from the kitchen. We are invited to take a seat as does our hostess and then she begins to talk to us using her daughter, our guide Rosa, as an interpreter. She asks us where we are from, where we are staying and so forth until a small wooden table is also brought out from the kitchen and a small wooden box is set before us.

Rosa speaks with her mother for a few moments in Ixil and then explains to us that they would like to sell us some items that they have found in the fields. As her mother looks on, Rosa opens the box and begins showing us a variety of small jade hatchet heads, stone beads, and figurines made of jade, stone, or clay. She carefully hands them to us, one at a time, explaining their significance while the other children and ladies hiding in the wings slowly inch forward to get a better view of the action.

It is immediately obvious that the items that she is showing us are authentic pre-Columbian Mayan artifacts well over 500 years old and probably older. We take our time discussing each piece and its price, trying to decide which to buy and how much to pay. Rosa patiently transfers all of our questions to her mother. They converse in Ixil for a bit until Rosa gives us her mother's answer. Almost an hour later I have purchased a small jade hatchet head for less than ten dollars, Anna has bought a collection of beads and Ron has bought a few old Spanish coins. We would like to stay longer but there is an impatient group of young girls still waiting silently at the front door to take us to another house so we pay for our purchases, thank our hostesses, and depart with our group of guides to the next house.

25

THE ASHRAM, 1991

*As you return to the oneness, do not think
of it or be in awe of it. This is just another
way of separating from it. Simply merge
into truth, and allow it to surround you.*
LAO TSU

I BEGAN TO notice something new emerging in my
recovery. When I went home after work to take my
short rest, and again at night when I went to bed, I
found that my hands, both open palms, automatically
placed themselves directly over my heart. I noticed
that it was happening naturally, of its own accord, and
that it gave me a feeling of great peace and serenity,
so much so that I would lay there for an hour or more
soaking up as much of this new healing energy as I
could. I could actually feel an energy, a strong, peaceful energy channeling itself into me through my palms,

running through my nervous system and mind repairing all of the damage of the "over-wattage" I had experienced. It wasn't until years later that I found out I was spontaneously practicing Reiki on myself even before I had heard of the technique.

With the return of stability and clarity, an amazing new creative energy began to flow through me. First, there was the flood of words I found myself writing every night as I tried to capture the beauty and grandeur I experienced on the course. With the jolting experiences of the recent past receding I was experiencing the first fruits of tangible positive transformation. It was as if all my past karma and incorrect perceptions had been dissolved and replaced with something that was absolutely fresh and vibrantly alive.

Was that the "dark night of the soul" then that I had just passed through? Was that the intensive physical, mental and spiritual cleansing, the hardships and the difficulties that the soul supposedly has to go though in order to detach itself from the world and reach the light of union with the Creator? I wasn't sure, but it definitely felt like I had gone through something of that nature. And even though I wasn't seeing God, it did feel like I had achieved a certain amount of "the peace that passeth all understanding".

Maybe there is a primordial darkness inside all of us that has to be confronted in order to reach higher levels of consciousness. I had always had issues in my life but had avoided them because they were either too complex or vague and murky to be pinpointed and resolved. But due to the massive amount of pure consciousness injected into me, and via the intense purification process that followed, I had been forced to confront the actual demons of my own particular existence and karmic make up. Things that had been there all my life and had either consciously or unconsciously manipulated and restricted me in regards to what I could perceive, realize, and accomplish in life.

But now it was all gone, or at least greatly diminished. I was free at last from the mental, emotional, and spiritual programming I had lived with (perhaps been born with) and had been governing my perceptions, thoughts, actions and very existence ever since I was a child. And it was this experience that I had been searching for all of my life, the experience of living from an unprogrammed and unrestricted point of view. Something good *had* actually resulted from the course and the intense confusion and restructuring that followed. And with the difficult phases behind me, I was reaping the immense rewards of having survived them.

In addition to the writing, there was the painting I started that fall of 1991. Never a painter before, my evenings were now spent sitting in my room making frames by hand, covering them with canvas, and painting Native American motifs. Again, a little surprised by this new found talent, I would sit for hours each evening and bask in the new peaceful energy that was flowing out from somewhere deep inside of me creating beautiful pieces of art. And they actually sold! On campus and in town people admired them and actually paid money for them.

Next was the paper recycling program I started on campus. It all started out simple enough. One day as I was throwing away a large amount of scrap paper, as we did on a daily basis in the pressroom, I suddenly realized I was part of a problem I had previously blamed on others. It was an amazing realization, and in seeing it for the very first time, I knew I had to do something about it. Picking up the telephone, I called around until I found a recycling company that supplied us with waste containers, picked them up at the end of the month, and paid us in cash. So out of nowhere (remember, this was 1991 before recycling as we know it today) I designed and initiated the campus recycling program, one of the first in the area.

But the most important thing, the thing that really excited me, was that connection with the Divine I was establishing once again. I could feel it again. Early in the morning as I watched the sun rise, late at night in the stars above, and every single time I walked alone in the woods or even across the grounds of campus to work in the morning. It was still there, it was still amazing and it contained everything I ever wanted in life. Just to sit in the grass or alone at night in my room painting or writing and feel it all around me and streaming through me in pure, silent being was the feeling that I lived for now. There was absolutely nothing I could compare it to. Sometimes it was strong and sometimes it was faint but the more I "aligned" myself with its energy through my thoughts, the decisions I made, and my activities throughout the day, the more I felt it.

Moving into 1992 I finally felt whole again, alive like only a reprieved man can feel. I now felt a sense of calm excitement and anticipation instead of dread, fear, and confusion for the first time in years. Something new was happening. I could feel it. I didn't know exactly what it was, but I could definitely feel it coming. I was now keenly interested everyday to see what would happen next. And all I had to do was get out of the way and let it happen.

Having made peace with nearly three years of intense inner turmoil, I was ready to leave the ashram. Yes, it was time to leave. After everything that had happened to me, I felt a trust had been betrayed. I certainly didn't want to hold a grudge, but I felt that the ashram and its instructors had been teaching half-truths and I had been lucky to survive the blind spots in their knowledge. So now it was time to leave, I felt strong enough now. I had no idea what I was going to find when I left, but I had to leave. I had to find out what it would be like to leave the ashram and my self-paced recovery to rejoin the life that I had left almost three years before. I was curious to see what would happen when I left the ashram. Had I really learned anything? What would it be like to live out there again after all that I had been through? What was I going to do when I left? All of these questions were before me as I prepared to leave. A month or two more I remember thinking. A month or two more and I should be ready to leave.

26

THE IXIL TRIANGLE, GUATEMALA, 1999

Our life is our own possession and its benefit to us is very great. Regarding its dignity, even the honor of being emperor could not compare with it. Regarding its importance, even the wealth of possessing the world would not be exchanged for it.
YANG CHU

WE PASS THE afternoon in Chajul being led around town by a small group of uniformed Indian girls taking us from one house to the next. At each house the same ritual is followed; we are greeted by the mother or father of the family, chairs and a treasure chest are brought out, items are presented, prices are quoted and deals are made. When the entire adventure is over almost three hours later we have bought very little but the memories, we know, will last us a lifetime. Exiting from the last house we are urged on to the next by our small group of Mayan guides, but funds are low so we satisfy ourselves with those items which we have purchased, the adventure of it all, and a promise to return one day.

We are all hungry after all of the travel and excitement of the day so we go down to the food stalls that line the village square. At the largest and cleanest of the stalls we take seats and order beers. Looking up at the sky I can see that clouds have been rolling in and with them a steadily dropping temperature. I am beginning to feel sick too, with a bad stomachache and a headache coming on. I also feel kind of weak and disoriented. Somehow I manage to force down a beer and a lukewarm order of chicken in some kind of sauce while I maintain a conversation with Anna and Ron.

After our meal we walk around the village for a while until the coming darkness and a light sprinkle of rain force us back towards our hotel. This entire village is so small, so poor, so dilapidated and so far-flung from the reality that I have known even in Mexico, it's unnerving in a weird kind of way and, combined with the cold rain falling and my illness I can't help but feel a little depressed. Back in the damp, ice-cold hotel room I crawl into bed and read for a while then, feeling even worse than before, slip fully clothed between soiled sheets that I can only hope are free of fleas and lice.

I awake the next morning feeling a little better but still a bit tired and weak. What is it, something I ate?

Too much travel these last few months? Looking out the window and seeing the warm sun, I hop out of bed and wake up Anna and Ron. Eager to get out of the depressing hotel and into the brilliant sunshine we pack our bags, check out of the hotel, and walk down to the market located next to the church where we buy some peanuts, flat bread, and fruit to accompany the cheese that we are still carrying from Nebaj. We climb the stairs up to the courtyard in front of the church and sit sunning ourselves while we eat our breakfast and converse with a few local Indians.

Finishing breakfast we shoulder our packs and head south to the outskirts of Chajul looking for the secondary road that we are hoping to take to Cotzal. After a bit of searching and much asking we find it and set off at a brisk pace. The going is easy and the road well-marked so there are no real problems as we walk along except that I feel unusually tired and weak. Why do I feel so tired and weak still? My stomach isn't too bad so it couldn't be something I ate. I don't even feel physically sick anymore, just a general weakness that is keeping me from enjoying the beautiful day and lovely countryside we are walking through. After an hour or so I find myself lagging behind Anna and Ron who are walking along in high spirits. When we come to a fork in the road I feel so bad that I decide to take the shorter, easier road to Cotzal while they take the longer, tougher route over the hill that the guide book says has an excellent view of the surrounding countryside.

We part company promising to meet at the church in Cotzal. I figure it is another half-hour to the village on the road I am following so I try to keep a steady pace but find myself moving slowly, feeling more tired and depressed by the minute. A half-hour passes and still no sign of Cotzal. I feel like I am out in the middle of nowhere, that the road I am on is not the road to Cotzal, but a few minutes later I catch my first glimpse of Cotzal in the valley below. Sighting the village does wonders for my spirits but it is still another quarter mile to the outskirts of the village.

The village appears to be about two or three times larger than Chajul but still much smaller than Nebaj. It's also spread out over a group of small interconnecting ridges and gullies, which make it hard to find the correct road into the village center, so as I walk along I have to ask directions at every store I come across. At every store where I ask for directions, I also ask for a beer. I need a beer, and not because I'm thirsty (there's still lots of water left in my water bottle). I just need beer. I'm hot and tired and weak and sick and feeling alone in the world and I just need a beer to make it all go away. But I'm out of luck. Even though every store offers directions for reaching the center of the village and the church, I am also informed that the only places that sell beer are also downtown still another five or ten minute walk away. So I trudge on, not so much to meet Anna and Ron now, but just to find a beer.

About six blocks later the village starts to take shape and I feel like I'm getting close to the center. Two blocks after that I see the church rise from behind the closer buildings, but better yet I see a store displaying a Gallo beer sign. Suddenly my spirits are lifted and I half skip, half run to the store. Entering the store I ask for a beer and wait impatiently as the twelve-year-old girl goes behind a curtain and then into the dark recesses of the store. It seems like hours before she finally returns with my beer. Money already in my hand I throw it down on the counter, grab the open beer, take a long, greedy gulp then ask for a cigarette and light up. Grabbing my beer I finish it off before my cigarette is half-gone, order another beer, and take a seat on the stairs out front, already feeling a lot better.

I sit for another fifteen minutes slowly smoking and drinking a total of three beers before I feel like moving on towards the church and my rendezvous with Anna and Ron. And there they are a few minutes later when I finally reach the village square in front of the church. They arrived about ten minutes ago, ask what took me so long, and inform me they have already found Cotzal's one hotel. Seeing them improves my spirits even more so I buy another beer, take a seat, and light up a cigarette.

For the next two hours I sit with Anna and Ron in the center of Cotzal drinking beer after beer while they nurse down two or three. We then buy some fried chicken and french fries at a stand off the square. At about 3:00 PM we meet an Indian woman who invites us to her house to see some more relics so we leave the square and walk up to her house where the same procedure is repeated as in Chajul. Once again we buy a few small items and then go to our hotel where

I finally drop my pack and take a seat on the balcony behind the hotel.

This hotel is a big improvement over the one in Chajul and I feel so much better here. It is a small hotel with only four rooms, but it is light and airy and the back porch is an excellent place to get a little sun, a view of the bottom half of Cotzal and the small valley that lies below. Looking down over the village I can see that Cotzal is even more quaint and charming than either Chajul or Nebaj and also a little lower in elevation, which makes it a bit warmer. We all sit on the back porch for a while basking in the sun then go out to dinner at the only real restaurant we can find, a Chinese restaurant run by a Guatemalan, where we have an excellent dinner and a few more beers before returning to the hotel.

27

THE ASHRAM, 1992

Even as fire without fuel finds peace in its resting place, when thoughts become silence the soul finds peace in its own source. And when a mind, which longs for truth finds the peace of its own source, then the false inclinations cease which were the result of former actions done in the delusions of the senses. And as water becomes one with water, fire with fire, and air with air, so the mind becomes one with the Infinite mind and thus attains final freedom.

MAITRI UPANISHAD

IT MUST HAVE been sometime around March of 1992. It was around two or three in the morning and I was alone in my room on campus. It was a small room measuring approximately ten by twenty feet, complete with a small bed and closet, a sink, the few possessions I owned, and a small curtained window. The door was locked and I was sound asleep. Suddenly I felt a tap on my shoulder and awakened immediately. At first I thought it a bit strange that someone had been able to enter my locked room and was now tapping me on the shoulder but when I turned over and saw what was awaiting me I understood completely.

Towards the far end of the small room where the door was, the entire door, wall, and in fact that entire part of the room, was pulsating, vibrating and glowing like some kind of special effects scene created for a movie. The room itself, though visibly still the same size as before, suddenly felt as big as the entire universe and full of the most amazing energy. Strange as it might sound, I felt absolutely no fear; instead, I instinctively knew that the Divine had come. I was in wonder, no doubt about that. I was enthralled, speechless, amazed but at the same time enveloped in a feeling of serenity, great love and complete trust. It felt like I was standing in the middle of a large stadium and hundreds of thousands of people were there, focusing their positive energy on me, cheering, loving and supporting me.

I was, of course, totally surprised, greatly excited, and intensely aware of the magnitude of what was happening. How many times had I prayed to God over those last two and half years, over my lifetime? How many times had I wondered, had doubts or questions that had gone unanswered? And how many stories had I read or heard about God in church or in other places and then wondered if He-She-It actually existed and if He- She-It did exist, what He-She-It was really like? And now He was there, bigger than big, realer than real, and in my room standing, or rather floating around pulsating and wiping away all doubts, all fears, all questions and all insecurities with His mere presence. I must say "He" here because it was a male voice that I heard that night but in hearing it intimately knew that it could just as well have been a female voice or even a voice without gender.

Then I heard a voice, His voice, in a large, dynamic, yet perfectly soft, calm and clear tone say to me, "Eric, you've been having a problem and been asking for my help and so I have come." A bit startled at first I didn't want to believe what was happening but it was so real, so true that there was no way of denying it. Continuing, the Presence said, "I know about this problem you've been having Eric, that it is something that you don't understand, so I have come to explain it to you." "This is really happening," I remember telling myself in the midst of it all. "Me, Eric Bullard from Portland, Oregon in the presence of God, right here, right now, and after all that has happened!"

Sitting up in my bed now I could feel my entire body vibrating in unison with the pulsating, dull glow that was entering the room through the portal that had opened on the far wall. I was actually receiving and vibrating not only with that pulsating glow from the far end of the room, but also with that incredible voice that was speaking to me and into me, to the deepest reaches of my being. Totally entranced now I felt a strong current of energy, similar to what I had been receiving through my self Reiki treatments, though much stronger, coursing through my body and nervous system.

Suddenly a screen, a sort of television or movie screen, appeared about two feet in front of me. It was about twenty-four inches wide, eighteen inches tall and floating in the air just above head level. Even though my eyes were wide open I was seeing it not only with my eyes but also directly with my mind, which perceived it through my reopened third eye. On the screen there was an expansive treeless plain with a range of brown snow capped mountains in the distance and a small river coursing its way down from the mountains, out onto the plain.

Then the Voice began again: "You see Eric, this river before you is the river of your life. Every person alive has a Sacred River of life just like this one, a special course which I have given them to follow. As long as they follow that river, that course I have given to them in this life, they will receive my guidance and help and will be able to achieve understanding, peace and even fullness amidst the turmoil, inconsistencies and confusion of daily human life. But the moment one deviates from the course of their river, they go into darkness, confusion, and fear and lose the guiding light of My Presence, somewhat like a boat leaving the main current of a fast flow and going over the reeds on the bank and getting lost in the swamps and thickets. Then one is almost surely alone and there is little I can do to help them until they realize their error and return to the main current of the river."

I sat there rooted to the spot, breathing it all in through every pore of my being. I felt It in every molecule of every atom in my body and knew that it would never end, that I would never end either because I had never been created. I was that same Eternity I was seeing and experiencing and, as such, also had no beginning or end. Then the Voice asked, "Are there any questions or anything else that you might need at this time?"

I was being cradled by the Creator and Protector of all life. It felt so safe and completely free of doubt that I felt like everything (not only from the last three years but my entire life of searching) had finally been resolved. And questions or needs? Oh how I wish now that I had had the sense of mind to ask quite a few questions and ask for some favors, too, but I was so incredibly overawed by that Presence that I didn't even consider asking for more. I simply smiled, answered "no" and allowed myself to enjoy the great sense of love and resolution that was being bestowed upon me.

The screen slowly disappeared and my focus was brought to rest once again on the pulsating glow that was dancing around and filling the room. I waited a moment and the Voice began again. "Well then, if there are no questions I will go, but there are some things that I want you to know before I do go." "Yes, what would that be?" I managed to answer. "I want you to remember that I am always here and that I am always listening, willing and ready to help. I want you to remember this night, always, and how much I love you dearly. I desire for you only the best and brightest that life has to offer. I also want you to remember that if you ever need anything, anything at all, just ask and I will be there." And with those parting words the dull pulsating light and Presence that had filled the room for the last twenty minutes slowly dimmed and departed.

I sat there for a minute in complete awe, staring at the door and the wall that just a second before had been so alive with energy, love and light. Slowly I got out of my bed, astounded by what had just happened. I went over to the mirror that hung over the sink in my room, looked at myself, then slapped myself hard in the face three times to make sure I was really awake, living this and not merely dreaming. After that I splashed handful after handful of ice cold water on my face. "Holy cow", I remember saying to myself, "that was the One and Only." I couldn't believe what had just happened but, as I said, it was all so simple, so real and so undeniable that I had to. I went back over to my bed and sat there on the edge while a broad smile slowly took shape on my face. Two months later I left the ashram.

28

THE IXIL TRIANGLE, GUATEMALA, 1999

*Greater than the joys of heaven and earth,
greater still than dominions over the
worlds, is the joy of reaching the stream.*
LORD BUDDHA

THE NEXT TWO days turn out to be an interesting mixture of exploring Cotzal and an even deeper exploration of my own feelings and present situation. I'm still feeling sick and weak and I don't know why. Anna and Ron are excellent people and great traveling companions but I want to be alone now. While they take off on excursions to waterfalls or outlying coffee *fincas* I walk alone in the hills outside of Cotzal where I follow a small, clear running stream and listen to the birds in the surrounding trees.

In the afternoons I wander through town or go down to the store below the hotel and pluck away at the owner's guitar. While there he tells me stories about the war and a time when villagers lived in constant terror and seldom ventured out of their houses after dark for fear of becoming one of the numerous corpses that for years appeared almost every morning in the streets of town. When Anna and Ron return in the afternoon I go back to the store and buy enough beer to last me through the night.

After three days it's almost time to get moving again, but I'm not really sure where I'm going. Ron is heading to Guatemala City for a flight back to Holland. Anna will accompany him to Guatemala City then head off to Honduras and maybe as far south as Chile. I have some stuff stored back in Todos Santos and an even larger pile of stuff stored back in San Cristobal, but I have no idea where to go or what I'm going to do next.

The next morning Anna and Ron take off to see one last natural wonder while I stay behind nursing another hangover. Around noon I take another long walk along the stream on the outskirts of town, wander through town a bit, and decide to visit the church. I almost always visit the Catholic Church that sits in the center of each small town or village that I visit. I always find it to be a rewarding experience in one way or another. Most of these churches are two or three hundred years old. The architecture alone is worth the visit, but there is always something else besides that that makes it worth the visit. Sometimes it's the

Indians, watching them pray, the intensity and honesty with which they do it. Sometimes it's the paintings, sometimes it's the altar and sometimes it's just the silence. For I often find these old churches empty, or nearly so, and a certain silence reverberating there within. And I guess that is what's drawing me towards this church today.

Around noon I return to the town square and climb the three short steps to the church. It appears to be about 200 years old, at least, and completely empty except for an older gentleman seated near the altar as a guard. It's a small church but appears able to hold 100 worshippers comfortably and maybe up to 150 squeezed in for more important occasions. I take a quick look around and walk along the right-hand side of the chapel viewing the few small religious paintings and poems on the wall, slowly working my way towards the altar.

This is a simple church; the poverty of the area is not able to support the extravagant outpourings of art, flowers and candles that one sees in the churches of San Cristobal or Antigua. But arriving at the altar I see a few small vases of handpicked flowers and some small candles burning in front of the cross. There is also an almost life-sized statue of the Christ in a prone position in what looks to be the final throes of pain and death from the crucifixion. I have seen many statues similar to this one in almost all of the churches I have visited throughout Mexico and Guatemala, but I have never seen one so terribly mutilated and in pain as this one. I cannot help but see it as a direct reflection of all of the suffering experienced by this village.

I stand for a few minutes in front of the dying Christ before working my way back along the opposite side of the church. I pass a few more paintings, a small mural and then come upon something I cannot recognize or understand. Hundreds of hand-sized, white wooden crosses are nailed to the wall. Lined up in neat horizontal and vertical rows, they cover an area approximately five feet by twenty. Upon closer inspection I see that each cross has a name, a date, and something else written below. I take a few moments to read a few in their entirety and nearly fall back into one of the pews sitting behind me.

The crosses are testaments, reminders and gravestones to those that were disappeared during the war here in Cotzal: Maria Juarez Gomez, 14 years old, kidnapped and murdered, 1983; Juan Gonzales Gonzales, 32 years old, tortured and murdered, 1980; Guadalupe Perez Sanchez, 19 years old, raped, tortured and murdered, 1979; Pedro Fernandez Rojas, 63 years old, kidnapped and murdered, 1978; Salina Hernandez Diaz, 12 years old, murdered, 1976; Fernando Rodriguez Perez, 15 years old, kidnapped, tortured and murdered, 1981; and Carmen Garcia Santana, 42 years old, kidnapped, raped and murdered, 1982.

I sit for a few moments trying to register what I have just read before I return to reading the crosses. I must assure myself this is really true, not some terrible mistake. I take my time and slowly read each name, date, and the underlying information. I hear a few worshippers come through the church to light a candle, say a prayer, or leave some flowers. But I am oblivious to all except the 500 crosses in front of me.

An hour or so later when I finally finish reading every cross I take a seat in one of the pews in front of the crosses but keep my gaze fixed on the tragedy and sorrow that is written on the wall before me. It's hard to explain the magnitude and multitude of feelings that are running through my heart and mind as I sit there stunned, not only by the immensity and intensity of man's violent and evil nature, but by the sadness, loss, pain and suffering that has brought each of these crosses to this church. Innocent little children, little girls and women raped, tortured and killed. That's the hardest for me to cope with. It fills my heart with sadness to the bursting point and tears begin to well up in my eyes as I am enveloped by a sorrow made so much deeper, wider and real by the fact that I am in the very town, walking the very streets where all of this took place.

I sit a while longer, engulfed in the embodiment of pain and sadness before me and I think back on my own seemingly senseless life. I get up from the old wooden pew and make my way towards the entrance of the church where I stop in the doorway for a minute and look out over the town that was the scene of all of this violence. Suddenly my life and problems seem so small and insignificant in comparison to what I have just read. Suddenly I feel such a fool to have made so many stupid mistakes in my life, to have suffered so much as a result of my own foolishness. I then become acutely aware of all that I have demanded of God and the world over the years without ever considering how fortunate I already was or what I could give back. I look back over the last five, ten years and see nothing but confusion and ignorance masked by my own arrogance and self-deception. And then somehow, slowly, all of my sadness, pain, and confusion turn into a feeling of humility and that humility into a sense of silent strength and conviction. All of the sudden I feel something, something coming from far away. Something from the past, my past, something long forgotten, now remembered and returning to lift me up and carry me back to the home I left so many years ago.

It's the river, that Divine current of spirit I had unknowingly forsaken when I left the ashram and became so preoccupied with myself and the world again. But in the blink of an eye, in a blood stained church, in Cotzal, Guatemala, in pain, confusion, deep humility, and surrender, I'm back in its current and home again. It is everything and everyone, always and everywhere. Like a fool, I've been trying to engineer its course. But it doesn't care about our worries, desires and expectations; it will not change to meet our demands. No, it is up to us to learn the ways of its current and follow its course. For it knows only its own sweet flow and the ever-present call of the spirit, freedom, and the sea.

EPILOGUE

God made the rivers flow. They feel no weari-
ness, they cease not from flowing. They fly
swiftly like birds in the air. May the stream of
my life flow into the river of righteousness.
Loose the bonds of sin that bind me. Let not
the thread of my song be cut while I sing. And
let not my work end before its fulfillment.
RIG VEDA 11: 28

I DON'T REMEMBER when I first heard the term Kundalini, whether I had skimmed over it in a book or some magazine article, but I had a passing familiarity with the word before my experiences on the course of 1989. Had you asked me what Kundalini meant at that time I would not have been able to tell you anything concrete, except that it was some sort of spiritual concept, maybe something to do with chakras.

It wasn't until I left the ashram in 1992 and began a deep, methodical search for answers in local bookstores and libraries that I began to find books about Kundalini. In reading those books I started to get a better sense of what I had been dealing with the last three years of my life. David Frawley's book, *Ayurvedic Healing*, with a small section on Kundalini disorders was the first book I stumbled across that talked not only about the incredible power of Kundalini, but also the inherent dangers that lay therein. It was only a one-page description, but reading it was like figuring out Einstein's theory of relativity; it was the first time I had ever seen Kundalini identified and described in terms so consistent with my experience.

After that discovery I began to narrow my search (remember this was 1992, way before the Internet was a sophisticated research tool) and found a few more books with accurate information on Kundalini. I say "accurate information" because the term Kundalini is a lot like the terms "Love" and "God": there are as many people as there are opinions about them. In the case of actual Kundalini experiences and Kundalini awakenings, I found most of the information inaccurate to the point of being laughable. But every once in a while I would find a gem, a book containing legitimate Kundalini experiences rather than theoretical or philosophical guess work.

The second book I found was entitled *Kundalini, Evolution and Enlightenment*, edited by John White. It was a thick book and a bit overwhelming, but in Swami Rama's commentary on the *Awakening of Kundalini*, especially pages 33-40, I began to get a good idea just what happened to me on that course in 1989. I was also given valuable explanations and information on the profound impact on the individual that a Kundalini awakening can have.

But it wasn't until 1998 in Mexico City that I really found what I was looking for. Just off of the *zocalo* in a bookstore with a small section of books in English I came across a book entitled *Kundalini, the Evolutionary Energy in Man,* by an East Indian named Gopi Krishna. Picking up Gopi Krishna's book there in Mexico City and reading about his own Kundalini awakening and the problems he was forced to confront I found someone with whom I shared an almost identical experience. Like me, he had experienced a spontaneous Kundalini awakening, which at first was amazing but quickly turned into a nightmare that lasted for over fifteen years and changed his life forever.

It is called a "premature or unprepared" Kundalini awakening. According to tradition you are supposed to work closely (a lot closer than I was) with a qualified yogi who is able to guide you through the inevitable difficulties encountered along the way. Ideally it is a process that takes years rather than the short time span and intermittent contact that I and Gopi Krishna had. Such gurus are hard to find, especially these days. If one is lucky enough to find a proper guru, they will put you through an exhaustive physical, academic, and spiritual preparation before working with the Kundalini force.

But I don't regret the way the experience unfolded for me. On the contrary, I feel very fortunate to have had the experience. True, it would have been a lot easier and I would have gained a lot more out of the experience working with a qualified guru or yogi over a much greater span of time. But I consider myself so lucky to have had the experience at all, even as difficult and distorted as it was. I got an incredible glimpse into the Divine and the deeper reality beyond the superficial manifestations of the world.

When I finally left the ashram in May of 1992 and went back to Portland, Oregon, I tried to fit into the new world around me, but leaving the ashram was a lot harder than I had thought it would be. Thrown into a turbulent work-a-day world of finances, strict time schedules and technology I wasn't ready for, I quickly found myself disillusioned, disconnected from the Sacred, and having a very difficult time following the current of the river that had been so gracefully presented to me that special night two months before I left the ashram. That complete resolution that I had been granted diminished then simply disappeared and I realized I should have asked for more that evening as I sat on my bed in the ashram listening to that Sacred Voice. I should have asked more questions too, but most of all I should have asked Him to come back the next night or at least stay a little longer. But I didn't. And so as the weeks and months whirled by in Portland I found myself more and more lost as time went by. I felt that the Divine had abandoned me; little did I know that it was I who had abandoned the Divine. After two years I became so dispirited that I bought a one-way ticket to Mexico and disappeared.

I continued my search in Mexico but to little avail (except for Gopi Krishna's book that I had found in Mexico City). I had a lot of information and answers but no concrete ideas what to do next. Loneliness and frustration prevailed and I found myself becoming angry at the world as never before. After all, I had had the secrets of the world explained to me but they weren't working, at least not how I wanted them to. Where had I gone wrong, how had I left the path so eloquently presented to me? Feeling alone and confused I lapsed into a spiritual desperation that led to drink. The more I drank the further I moved away from the Sacred and the further away I moved from the Sacred the more I drank.

It wasn't until that little blood-stained church in Cotzal that I finally got the slap in the face I so desperately needed to awaken from the self-pity, self-delusion, and anger I had been nurturing since I left the ashram. After that trip to Guatemala I went back to San Cristobal, quit drinking, and started to re-center myself in spiritual principles and practices. After a few years in San Cristobal I bought another one-way plane ticket, but this time it was to India.

In India, and later in Nepal, I read and expanded upon my spiritual program. I visited ashrams and gompas, temples and shrines, and studied in many of these places as I worked to expand my understanding of Kundalini and the Sacred in all of its manifestations.

Slowly but surely I was able to recapture a sense of the Sacred River and my place in the world again. Arriving at the Boudhanath Stupa just outside Kathmandu in the spring of 2007, I finally realized what the next step was for me. I was supposed to go back to the United States and write about my experience at the ashram. I had actually started a book during those last few years in Mexico but it was a rough sketch and I put it on hold while I continued my search for answers, most of which you are now reading.

I will never doubt the world of incredible peace, beauty, and coherence I first discovered in the summer of 1989, nor will I ever doubt the presence of that Benevolent Force that visited me in the spring of 1992. What I would sometimes prefer to forget are the personal demons and overwhelming fear that plagued me for so many years. But I cannot do that for I know they are as true and as real, at least in the relative-material world, as the peace and beauty I experienced. The question then is this: if there is a God, a positive force regulating everything for the good of all, as it always has been, why, or rather how can there be such terrible forces in mankind and the world? An excellent question and one that not only I have asked myself, but one that has been asked throughout the ages by untold millions. "The Eternal Search for the Ultimate Reality" could be one way of putting it. And the truth of the matter is that I don't really know the answer. But I can always refer back to what that Benevolent Force told me as I sat there on my bed in wonder two months before leaving the ashram for the last time.

There is a plan, a master plan for each and every one of us and all of life. As it was portrayed to me it is a beautiful, sparkling river pure, deep, clear, and true. It is the discovery of this river within ourselves, this fountain of knowledge, wisdom, humility and surrender to Divine grace that will lead us to a happiness, an understanding, a peace and a tranquility that can never be damaged or diminished. I think Ralph Waldo Emerson said it very well when he said, "A little consideration of what takes place around us every day would show us that a higher law than that of our own will regulates events; that our painful labors are very unnecessary and altogether fruitless; that only in our easy, simple, spontaneous action are we strong, and by contenting ourselves with obedience we become Divine. Belief and love, a believing love will relieve us of a vast load of care. There is a soul at the center of nature, and over the will of every man, so that none of us can wrong the universe. It has so infused its strong enchantment into nature that we prosper when we accept its advice; and when we struggle to wound its creatures, our hands are glued to our sides, or they beat our own breasts."

In retrospect I really have no one but myself to blame for all that happened those last two and a half years in the ashram. I was the one who trusted so completely my life, my mind, my soul and my well-being to others and then refused to see the warning signs of impending disaster. It was simply a case of my own ignorance compounded by something that I thought was very simple and beautiful which snowballed into something that I was unable to control or comprehend. A good example is Mickey Mouse in the movie *Fantasia*, when he learns a little magic and is able to control inanimate objects, which in the end turn against him and he is powerless to do anything about it because the magic which he has learned is incomplete. And that was basically what happened in my case. I got a really good glimpse of the big picture but unfortunately it was only partial and not complete. And as I said earlier, when one is dealing with things of this nature, enlightenment, Kundalini, supernatural powers and so on, partial knowledge can be even more dangerous than complete ignorance.

I guess the biggest thing that I have learned from all of this, besides the knowledge of the river, is the depth and magnitude of not only my own ignorance but that of mankind. It is amazing how much in the dark we really are in regards to what is out there and available to us. It is my most anxious hope that we as individuals, and collectively as a planet someday realize not only the depth of our ignorance but also, and more importantly, the key to safely unlock the power and wisdom of the Kundalini force in order to show us the way to true wisdom, true peace, true love and ultimate coherence. Looking at the world these days, a world so out of control with violence, pollution, anger and pain it would be too easy to discount the fact that there is a force silently waiting within us all that is capable of curing all of these problems and much more. But there it is, waiting silently and patiently to be unleashed in a cohesive, positive manner.

These days when I get a little tired, confused, or irritated with the world that I see around me I still find myself retreating into nature, into the mountains, into the trees and silence that is always there. Once outside of the noise and confusion of the city I walk until I find a barren mountain ridge or lone tree that speaks to my soul. Arriving, I usually take a seat, close my eyes, and listen to the silence while it gently takes me back to a time, a memory, and a source that I all too often forget: sitting alone on my bed back in the ashram listening to the Voice of All Creation while it gently explains the secrets of life to me in a beautiful, soft whisper of song.

Kundalini: Kundalini is the Eastern religious or spiritual tradition of an internal energy that can be awakened in order to purify the individual and facilitate a state of Yoga or complete union with the Divine. For most people it lays dormant at the base of the spine, a small fraction or reflection which serves to maintain our normal, everyday nervous system activities. The power of Kundalini can be awakened through pranayama, meditation, or even temporarily through the use of drugs such as L.S.D. In fact, many modern day recreational drugs work by artificially stimulating Kundalini. Kundalini is not something to be toyed with. It can be aroused artificially, prematurely, or turned on too strong which can result in serious illness, insanity, or even death.

Recommended Reading

1. **Frawley, David, O.M.D.** *Ayurvedic Healing; A Comprehensive Guide.* **Passage Press, 1989.**

   A good perspective and explanation of the theories, principles, and various therapies of the Ayurvedic healthcare system. Of special interest is Chapter 10 on conditions involving the mind, meditation disorders, and Kundalini.

2. **Jung, C.G.** *The Psychology of Kundalini Yoga.* **Princeton University Press, 1996**

   Notes from a series of lectures given in 1932 by the famous psychologist, Dr. Carl Jung, in Zurich on Kundalini and higher states of consciousness.

3. **Krishna, Gopi. Kundalini (with commentary by James Hillman).** *The Evolutionary Energy in Man.* **Shambhala Publications, Inc., 1997**

   A must-read for anyone interested in the phenomenon of Kundalini and what can happen when that force is awakened without proper preparation.

4. Krishna, Gopi. *Living with Kundalini.* Shambhala Publications, Inc., 1993
   Gopi Krishna's autobiography and an in-depth look into his own personal Kundalini experience.

5. Krishna, Gopi. *The Awakening of Kundalini.* Institute for Consciousness Research and Kundalini Research Foundation, Ltd., 1975
   More brilliant insight and commentary by Gopi Krishna on the power and mystery of the Kundalini force.

6. Patanjali, (with commentary by Prabhavananda, Swami and Christopher Isherwood). *How to Know God, The Yoga Aphorisms of Patanjali.* Vedanta press, 1953
   An in-depth look into and study of the Yoga Sutras of Patanjali.

7. Whatmore, Mark; Eltringham, Peter. *Guatemala and Belize, The Rough Guide.* Rough Guides Ltd., 1994
   A great guide to the Guatemalan highlands with historical information.

8. White, John (ed.). *Kundalini, Evolution and Enlightenment.* Paragon House Publishers, 1990
   A vast collection of commentaries on Kundalini and its different aspects by leading experts in the field including Shri Chinmoy, Ken Wilbur, Sri Aurobindo, Swami Muktanada, and many others.

9. **Wright, Richard. *Among the Maya*. Grove Press, 1989**

   A good, comprehensive overview of the Maya, their history and their culture in southern Mexico and Guatemala.

10. **(Various authors). *The Upanishads.***

    The Upanishads are a set of Hindi spiritual writings, the oldest of which were composed between 800 and 400 B.C. The spirit of the Upanishads can be compared to that of the New Testament.

EPIGRAPH SOURCES

1. Eihei Dogen quoted from The Tao of Abundance by Laurence G. Boldt, Penguin Compass Publishers, 1999.
2. Marcel Proust quoted from La Prisonniere by Marcel Proust, French and European Publications Inc., 1987.
3. William James quoted from Varieties of Religious Experience by William James, CreateSpace Independent Publishing Platform, 2009.
4. Rabbi Nachman of Bratzlav quoted an from unknown source.
5. Edgar Mitchell quoted from The Institute of Noetic Sciences, Petaluma, California, source material.
6. Yoga Kundalini Upanishad quoted from the Yoga Kundalini Upanishad, various publishers.
7. Chuang Tzu quoted from The Tao of Abundance by Laurence G. Boldt, Penguin Compass Publishers, 1999.
8. Shankara's Crest Jewel of Discrimination quoted from Shankara's Crest Jewel of Discrimination,

translated by Swami Prabhavananda and Christopher Isherwood, Vedanta Press, 1947.

9. William Blake quoted from an unknown source.

10. Savitri, Book VII, Canto 5 quoted from Savitri: A Legend and a Symbol, Sri Aurobindo, Sri Aurobindo Ashram Publications, 1948.

11. Gopi Krishna quoted from Kundalini, The Evolutionary Energy in Man by Gopi Krishna, Shambhala Publications, Inc., 1997.

12. Carl Jung (chapter 10) quoted from The Tibetan Book of the Dead, Oxford University Press, 2000.

13. The Sacred Sign of the Snake, unpublished manuscript.

14. Swami Rama quoted from Kundalini, Evolution and Enlightenment edited by John White, Paragon Press, 1990.

15. The Supreme Teaching quoted from an unknown source.

16. The Laughing River of Dragon Fire, unpublished manuscript.

17. The Upanishads quoted from the Upanishads, various publishers.

18. The Dhammapada quoted from the Dhammapada, various publishers.

19. Carl Jung (chapter 17) quoted from Memories, Dreams, Reflections, recorded and edited by Aniela Jaffe, Random House, Inc., 1961.

20. The Bhagavad Gita quoted from the Bhagavad Gita, various publishers.

21. Katha Upanishad quoted from the Upanishads, various publishers.

22. Ernest Holmes quoted from The Science of the Mind by Ernest Holmes, Tarcher-Penguin Publishing, 1926.

23. Huai Nan Tzu quoted from The Tao of Abundance by Laurence G. Boldt, Penguin Compass Publishers, 1999.

24. Katha Upanishad quoted from The Upanishads, various publishers.

25. Ranier Maria Rilke quoted from an unknown source.

26. Herbert Otto quoted from an unknown source.

27. Lao Tzu quoted from The Tao of Abundance by Laurence G. Boldt, Penguin Compass Publishers, 1999.

28. Yang Chu quoted from an unknown source.

29. Maitri Upanishad quoted from The Upanishads, various publishers.

30. Lord Buddha quoted from the Dhammapada, various publishers.

31. The Rig Veda quoted from the Rig Veda, various publishers.

32. Ralph Waldo Emerson quote from Nature and other writings, Ralph Waldo Emerson, Shambhala Publications, Inc., 1994.

ACKNOWLEDGEMENTS

I WOULD LIKE to personally thank the following people, institutions, and companies without whose help this work might never have come to completion:

Sheri Davidson of Metropolitan Family Services in Portland, Oregon for important clarification, guidance, and help throughout 1992 and 1993. Annemiek Kroone for the same, and so much more, including preliminary reviews, love, and constructive criticism during 1998 and 1999. Polo and Nicolasa Mendoza for letting me be part of the family. Grupo Cambio de Vida and all the boys there on Calle Real de Guadalupe in San Cristobal de las Casas, Chiapas, Mexico, during the years 2000 through 2003. Alberto Gordillo Gordillo of San Cristobal de las Casas, for technical assistance and computer maintenance way beyond the call of duty during the years 2000 through 2004. Miriam Cano Garcia of San Cristobal de las Casas for incredible amounts of love and understanding. Matthew Monte for inspiration, spiritual maintenance, and feedback in India during August and September of 2005. Norbu and Dolma Gyaltsen of the Mahabaudha guesthouse in Spiti Valley, India. Rinpoche Lochen Tulku of Ki Monastery, India and all the lamas and monks, big and small, for refuge and understanding during the summer of 2006. Ani Maya, Soam, and all of the nuns at Nagi Gompa nunnery in Shivapuri National Park, Nepal, The Alano Club of Portland, Oregon, Bob Brand, Kevin Reid, Claire Ruby Foster, and Gopi Krishna for important clarification (more than he will ever know or I can possibly say). And last but not least, Matthew Monte (again) for editing the manuscript, Travis Crane at CreateSpace Publishing, and anyone I might have forgotten along the way.

ABOUT THE AUTHOR

ERIC BULLARD WAS born and raised in Portland, Oregon. He studied humanistic psychology and meditation with Randy Revell, Maharishi Mahesh Yogi, and Deepak Chopra, among others. In 1985 he entered into a Hindu ashram where he spent the majority of the next seven years studying Ayurveda and deep meditation techniques. Moving to Mexico in 1994, he spent the next eleven years grounding himself in that experience while living and working with the Highland Maya tribes of Southern Mexico and Northern Guatemala. Leaving Mexico in 2005, he made a pilgrimage to the Indian and Nepalese Himalayas to continue studies in meditation, Ayurveda, and Tibetan Buddhism. Eric lived, studied, and taught in various Tibetan Buddhist monasteries over the next two and a half years. He now divides his time between Portland, Oregon and San Cristobal de las Casas, Mexico where he continues his work and writing.

www.theashramericbullard.com

Made in the USA
Charleston, SC
08 January 2015